NOT INTUITIVELY OBVIOUS

TRANSITION
TO THE PROFESSIONAL
WORK ENVIRONMENT

J. A. RODRÍGUEZ Jr.

Library of Congress Control Number: 2009901837
ISBN: Hardcover   978-1-4415-1542-1
                     Softcover   978-1-4415-1541-4

To order additional copies of this book, contact:
Xlibris Corporation
1-888-795-4274
www.Xlibris.com
Orders@Xlibris.com
58563

CONTENTS

DEDICATION

To my son, Isaac, and my daughter, Kayla, as they enter the professional working environment. This dedication also extends to my wife, family, and friends, who always seem to make the world a better place, and to the devoted military families, who sacrifice it all every day so that I can have the freedom to share this life-long experience.

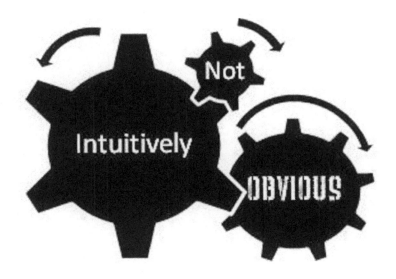

BOOK ONE

Transition to Professional

Professional Wisdom:

Knowing when to lead and when to follow; when to carefully listen and when to thoughtfully speak; when to seek assistance and when to offer guidance; and most importantly, knowing how to effectively approach it all.

PREFACE

Not Intuitively Obvious: Transition to the Professional Work Environment is a book directed at one goal: to provide you with the knowledge to excel in the professional work environment without the requisite of devoting many years learning from mistakes. This priceless knowledge and eventual wisdom is *not intuitively obvious* and is offered to you from the memoirs of seasoned professionals, who have learned these lessons through years of experience, trials, tribulations, and hardships.

This book will teach you how to attain expectation fulfillment and manage the organizational perceptions that guide your professional destiny and is written from two perspectives: (1) a senior management perspective that details management thought processes and expectations of employees and (2) an employee's perspective that sheds light on the reasons why some professionals rarely advance up the corporate ladder while others ascend successfully.

Your challenges, situational circumstances, and your conditions will be different; nonetheless, the concepts of integrity, ethics, perception management, performance and expectation fulfillment, respect for others, and respect for your company are everlasting. Apply the approaches described in this book, and you will increase your chances of succeeding in your professional endeavors. During economically strained times, only those informed professionals who master the noted approaches are offered the best opportunity to secure and preserve their jobs within organizations.

Your mind-set paves the road for and determines the strength of your career's foundational structure.

CHAPTER 1

Establishing Your Mind-set, Your Foundation

Allowing yourself to succeed is the keystone to achieving your career goals. The concept sounds simple, yet most professionals do not reach their full potential simply because they do not realize that a proper mind-set must precede the establishment of career goals. How you approach and live your life has a major impact on how you perform and achieve success at work. How you view your role in the organization, in your department, and in your particular group predetermines your path whether you realize it or not. Establishing your mind-set, your foundation early, can make the difference between wishing away your life and willing your ambitions toward reality.

Your mind-set is driven by your perspective or by the way you choose to view the world. Several of the mind-sets listed are discussed in subsequent chapters and are incorporated to emphasize their importance as a foundational requirement. The underpinning viewpoints are broad, have proven to be invaluable in establishing and maintaining a winning attitude, and are quintessential to drafting a road map for success:

- Think highly of yourself, dress the part, have the confidence that you can accomplish anything without crossing the line into arrogance. Remain confident without projecting the impression that you are a star in your own mind.

  o There are many involuntary actions that provide others with clues as to how you view yourself. Among these are your posture, the way you carry yourself, your expressions, your reactions, your overall demeanor and behavior, your verbal inflections, your attire, and the way you respond to others in person. True feelings are exposed to the trained eye through your involuntary actions.

o   Believing in yourself and liking who you are will manifest into those positive impressions, which require neither explanation nor description. The results of these actions are automatic; the benefits of which are immediately visible.

- Protect your reputation and that of the organization, earn respect; both actions help facilitate your success.

o   Reputation is the river that provisions life into a career. It is the way that leads to opportunity and the key card to the door of success. Reputation is, by far, the most important measuring vehicle in the professional working environment. Protect your reputation by tirelessly improving it, by defending it from unjustified raids, by repairing it in times of indiscretion. Realize that it takes a lifetime of properly executed actions to build and maintain an impeccable reputation and only one inappropriate action to destroy it. The rebuild process is much more laborious and taxing than the build process. There are actions that can damage a reputation beyond repair. A reputation built on credibility, sincerity, and respect is difficult to subdue. Focus on building and reinforcing your reputation, and you will not need to ponder about the strategies for repair.

o   The protection of your organization's reputation is also of most importance as customers typically only engage in business ventures with entities that have reputations beyond reproach. Your job security highly depends on the level of confidence customers perceive on your organization's reputation.

- The professional work environment is business and not personal. Leave the imposing emotions and personal issues at home.

o   Publically traded corporations primarily exist for two reasons: to generate a net profit from investment and to reward investors for their trust in the organization. The overwhelming

---

drivers in most business decisions are financially based. Investors demand performance, stability, and predictability. Publically traded corporations that base their business decisions on emotions are viewed as investment liabilities and are shunted by investors. Organizations naturally reflect these same expectations on their employees as well. Nothing is generally personal, just business. Realize that most employment terminations are carried out primary because the business views their partnership with the affected employees as a liability rather than as an investment.

o   The professional workplace is not the environment to display your strong emotions and introduce your personal issues. These mangos are not worth the climb. Success is speckled with preparations and opportunities, not detractors and liabilities.

- A positive attitude is contagious and so is a negative one. Wear a smile; you will utilize less face muscles than a frown. Your job security will significantly improve by projecting a positive attitude. The alternative does not offer career enhancing opportunities.

o   Investors carefully evaluate organizations to determine culture and its relation to optimism. An organization that is reported to be suffering from morale issues is considered to be a liability through the perception of volatility. Morale issues are an indicator of management's inability to motivate and invigorate the workforce. These types of issues affect productivity that leads to not meeting customer expectations that leads to loss of future work that leads to perceptions of instability that leads to layoffs that leads to lack of investor confidence that leads to the eventual demise of the organization if left unchecked.

o   Morale issues typically manifest themselves through negative attitudes that employees display in the work environment. Attitudes, positive or negative, are contagious and are the primary driver of culture behavior. Management is tasked with eliminating and/or mitigating all liabilities including those that surface through employee morale. Your ability to maintain a positive attitude at all times, regardless of the situation, will pay dividends as you will be viewed as an asset rather than as a liability in the eyes of the organization. Additionally, a positive attitude is one of the requirements and sought-after traits in the offering of promotional opportunities. Organizations generally promote employees to management positions, in part, for their ability to prevent, indentify, and correct morale issues within the work environment.

- Focus on teamwork; all other approaches will fail.

  - Imagine a stormy ocean with high seas and a ship crested upon the formidable swells that pass over the deck taunting its power. The ship's mast and deck is being indiscriminately tattooed by lightning, hail, and unrelenting winds. Imagine this ship carrying a crew uncertain of its fate yet confident and dependent of the ship's steel structure for survival. Imagine the ship equally dependent upon the crew's anticipatory preparation, expertise, determination, decision-making capabilities in the time of crisis, emergency response preparedness, and their insurmountable ability to harness the power generated by team synergy to forge forward to calmer seas. Imagine the likelihood of survival and the probability of success if the crew and the ship sailed as one.
  - Shift gears and imagine the same crisis with one exception: crew members are focused on themselves and their own survival where the survival of the rest and that of the ship are a distant consideration. Imagine the likelihood of survival and probability of success under this plan.
  - There is no greater force in the professional work environment than the force generated by motivated employees working in effective teams toward a unified and common purpose. Teamwork is not an option; it is a requirement of survival for the organization and the employee. Corporations view employees that embrace and thrive in team environments as star employees eligible for the benefits generally associated with the recognition. Corporations view employees that undertake leadership roles in teams through diplomacy, perceptual election, and buy-in as front-runners for the management card.

- Sincerely believe that most people are good and work toward performing the best job possible.

  o Most professionals generally desire to grow, expand their horizons, and leave at the end of the day with a feeling of accomplishment and self-worth. All too often, we, as human beings, allow perceptions or filters to interfere with our view of another person's intents.

  o Establish a foundational belief that most professionals commence their workday looking forward to performing the best job possible, and all other filters will fade. This approach helps you view the positives in otherwise stressful situations.

  o Offer your colleagues the benefit of doubt.

- Treat everyone with respect even during those times when you feel the person or the organization is not deserving of this courtesy. It is possible to disagree; be respectful and reach consensus.

  o You have a high probability of success justifying reasons for certain business process variations such as those associated with a slip in schedule or a cost overrun. There is never an acceptable reason for behaving in a disrespectful manner in the eyes of the organization regardless of the situation. Disrespectful behavior adversely affects your reputation and your employer's view of your ability to arrive at effective business solutions when the chips are down. Treat everyone with respect always. Your reputation will reap the valuable benefits.

  o The salient factor is how the other party views your communication and not how you intended the other party to receive it.

- People typically forget the issues but rarely forget your approach and behavior.

  o Approaches to situations that focus on the facts of the issues rather than on emotions will yield better results. All too often, employees are disciplined by their employers because of the approach elected to solve an issue. Natural behavioral defense mechanisms focus on protection and preservation of self. The goal of this defense mechanism is to divert attention from the facts over to the actions taken to resolve the issue. Typically, this translates to a mugging of the approach rather than an evaluation of the situational facts.

o   Remember to always consider your approach to situations; and purposefully follow protocol, professional courtesy, and respectful overtures in solving issues. Organizations view the concept of collateral damage as an indicator of an employee's ability to resolve issues and the employee's potential candidacy for a leadership role. The lower the collateral damage generated from your approach, the higher you are regarded. Collateral damage is viewed by organizations as a profit detractor because of the time and money involved in picking up the pieces resulting from the event.

o   Work to limit collateral damage, focus on an amenable approach, and remember that your actions encircle a life of their own.

•   You are responsible for your career.

o   Organizations hire employees to perform work that supports their vision and mission. The role of your employer is to ensure you have the required guidance and work environment to effectively perform your duties at the highest levels in support of the organization's commitments to its customers. Good employers offer professional development opportunities. Great employers help facilitate the appropriation of these opportunities by additionally offering flexible work schedules, educational assistance, and mentorship. These are all benefits, not rights. Your employer owes you nothing more than described in the memorandum of understanding you both signed at the onset of your business relationship.

o   Professional advancement and career fulfillment comes at the expense of your willingness to focus on taking responsibility for your career. Establishing this mind-set early in your career will provide you with a deeper perspective into the approaches required to assure your success. It is your career. Grab it by the horns.

- When you are starting a career, there are no conflicting conveniences. Establish and focus on your career goals and eliminate distractions.

  o One of the most difficult challenges a professional faces is the prioritization of what is truly important. This list manifests itself in as many variations as there are people on this earth. There are, however, a few guiding principles that can help you decide and, consequently, determine your best path. First decide if you want to start a professional career. If the answer is no, you are all set. No further action is required. If the answer is yes, you must commit to not impose conflicting conveniences upon yourself. Conflicting conveniences are those things that make you feel good but do not help in the advancement of your career. Their presence creates distractions. Distractions alter focus. Focus issues are apparent to your organization and derail your career opportunities.

  o Help identify conflicting conveniences by remaining honest with yourself and noting that most of the conveniences you give up now will return with dividends during a successful professional career.

  o Note that all actions and inactions manifest themselves in consequences. The type of consequence, good or not good, depends on your decisional choices.

- Always realize and remember your role in every situation.

  o Viewpoints, approaches, and personalities aside, your situational awareness is critical to affecting how your behavior is judged by your management. As a new professional member of the team, you are assigned a role that is often not disclosed. Your role is typically inferred or expected as a matter of course and varies greatly with the culture of the organization. You are typically viewed as the bearer of fresh ideas and innovative approaches. You are typically expected to be enthusiastic, energetic, willing to learn, and accepting of direction.

  o Recognize your role within the organization's culture. Behave and respond in such a way as to conform to your boss's expectations.

Develop effective approaches suitable for the situation and establish your own legacy. Organizations are typically not built to readily accept dramatic change. Be patient, the partnerships you form will help you implement the changes necessary to help lead the organization to a new performance level.

- Focus on helping the organization succeed; your success will materialize as a result.

  o Address and redefine the *me* concept. The *we* and *us* concepts are better suited for the professional work environment.
  o Realize that the only passageway to your success is through the corridors leading to the success of the organization.
  o Perform with the intention, not to improve yourself, rather to improve the organization. Your development and recognition will not be far behind.

- Conduct yourself as if everyone has a watchful eye on you even if you believe this action is not possible. This behavior approach projects integrity and ethical conduct. The reality is that someone is watching all the time.

  o Security surveillance systems, physical security systems, and IT security systems are examples of the many surveillance resources employers have available at their disposal to assure their interests are protected.
  o Nontraditional surveillance systems are also part of the arsenal. These include interested employees that notice the exact time other employees arrive at work, depart and return from lunch, and end their workday. Additionally, these employees notice how much time is devoted by other employees to the performance of their job. The concept of teamwork is weakened when teammates have the impression that a fellow teammate is not pulling his or her own weight.
  o The one sure way to not have to worry about who is watching is to behave in such a manner as if everyone is watching. This behavior is required, not simply expected. Realize that the actions you choose now can and will affect your career,

especially if your job requires a security clearance. Security-sensitive positions are sensitive to your behavior inside and outside of the work environment. A lapse in judgment including being in the wrong place at the wrong time may cost you your security-sensitive position.

- Assume that all your communications are public. Protect yourself and your organization.

    o Every e-mail and every memo you transmit and every conversation you have are open to all within your organization for scrutiny. Sometimes, these communications are open to outside parties as well. The courts are full of cases where organizational communication vehicles are the star witness. Recall that the salient factor is how your message is perceived and not how you intended it to be received.

    o Demonstrate discretion when you communicate, especially in writing. Written communications have a life expectancy beyond that which is expected, typically forever. The words you write could have an adverse effect on you and the organization. Placing your employer at risk through careless communications is not advisable. When in doubt, seek your boss's advice.

- Always look to contribute significantly; that is why you are financially compensated.

    o The basic premise for your employment is that you agree to provide your expertise in support of the organization.

    o The organization pays you for the productivity and benefit it expects to attain from your efforts.

    o Realize that there are typically no other reasons for your employment.

- All battles cannot be fought today but, with the right approach, can be fought tomorrow.

    o Wisdom, in part, is the realization of why and how. Longevity constitutes within the realization of when.

- There will be times in your career when you will need to step back and regroup. It is not wise to enter into a heated professional engagement when the outcome is likely to end in defeat. Passion has a place in the professional environment and is the driver for success. Passion can also be a hindrance when it obscures your view of the big picture. Keep passion in check and learn to skillfully release it appropriately.

- Listen to others; they are telling you what is important.

  - One of the most difficult skill sets to attain is the ability to listen. Introverts tend to be better listeners than extroverts.
  - Listening is a basic skill set essential to professional growth. Mastering this skill allows for the better understanding of issues, for the establishment of perspective, and for the transference of what is truly important.

- Attempt to walk in the shoes of others; look at the situation from their perspective.

  - As a general rule, your perspective represents a small subset of the overall picture. True understanding is derived from gathering, organizing, processing, and analyzing information that originates from several sources and stakeholders.
  - Your ability to objectively arrive at your perspective is an attribute organizations seek when your perspective is derived from an inclusive viewpoint.
  - Consider the impact your suggestions or decisions will have on the organization. Remain focused on the fact that your actions affect more than your department. They affect the organization. In this regard, take a broad view of the issue before deciding on a course of action.

- Socialize your ideas.

  - Socialization is an elemental and essential part of the teamwork concept.

- o Discuss the possibilities individually with others and receive feedback. The feedback you receive is an invaluable insight into how that person views your suggestion for improvement or approach.
- o Ask for their suggestions on your proposal early. The result will be rewarding.
- o Do give credit to those who helped you arrive at your suggestions publically. Share your appreciation with their bosses.
- o Approaches that involve inclusion work much better than approaches that involve exclusion.

- • Professional priorities in order of preference:

  - o Integrity
  - o Ethics
  - o Commitment
  - o Relationships
  - o Safety/Quality of Work/Quantity of Work

- • Defeat is not an option, only a possibility available to those who expect it.

  - o Set a foundational value that you will not accept defeat as one of the viable options in your life and career.
  - o Setbacks are not considered defeats if you harvest the lessons learned and impart these lessons into the discernable and beneficial concept called experience.
  - o Rather than wallow in negative feelings after a perceived harmful event, search, instead, for the buried treasure of knowledge within and add rigidity to your foundation. Extract the positive, expunge the negative.
  - o Expectations of defeat will materialize during your professional career. Neutralize these thoughts and focus on the lesson learned paving the way to success.

---❖—

*If you look and sound professional,
you probably are.*

—❖—

Chapter 2

First Impressions,
a Hiring Manager's Perspective

Many great books are available that propose approaches to establishing positive first impressions and prepare you for the job interview process. Rather than summarize that advice here, this chapter focuses on how the hiring manager views interviewees and the behavior that interviewee should exhibit to exceed most manager expectations. Exceeding the hiring manager's expectations significantly increases the probability of a job offer. Oftentimes, fully qualified candidates are not offered the job because the hiring manager or other interview team member feels the interviewee is not a good *fit* for the organization. Hiring managers desperately desire to acquire the services of low-maintenance, team-focused, high-performing employees who will achieve expeditious acceptance from the rest of the team. The concept of *fit for the team* is vague and varies widely from organization to organization; each defines what taboo is and what taboo is not. It is for this reason that the interview candidate must possess a deep understanding of the foundational reason for all interviews and must apply a time-tested and proven approach to every interview opportunity.

What is the foundational reason for a job interview? Job openings occur when an organization has more work than resources to complete the work. This imbalance creates a need. The need creates a job opening. The job opening initiates the recruitment process. The recruitment process leads to the careful selection of potential candidates. The down selection of potential candidates leads to the interview process. The interview process is the last opportunity for the hiring manager to evaluate a candidate before hire. A job candidate applying for a professional position is viewed as a potential resource that possesses the capability to complete the required work in exchange for financial compensation. The expectations are that the interviewee will not require significant organizational resources to acclimate to the job at hand. Time is money, and money is an investment for the organization. The organization views all investments the same way. Investments must either produce a profit or produce another vehicle that produces a profit. At the end of the day, all investments are expected to produce financial gain for the stockholders of the organization.

What is the time-tested and proven approach that you must understand before an interview? Bottom line: understand how a hiring manager views you and the governing traits most hiring managers value during an interview. A hiring manager views you as a potential investment. Given the same professional qualifications, the hiring manager must ascertain from the multiple applicants, which one has the right approach, the right attitude, and the right conviction to help catapult the organization ahead of its competitors. Hiring managers look for the following traits in young professionals:

- Genuine enthusiasm, confidence in speaking, team-oriented responses
- Courtesy

  o Arrive ten to twenty minutes early.
  o Rise anytime anyone enters the interview room; extend a greeting.
  o Offer a firm handshake, and make eye-to-eye contact.
  o Silence personal electronic equipment, especially your cell phone.
  o Demonstrate gratitude for the opportunity.

- Professional attire and communications

  o Dress to impress.
  o Communicate to impress.

- Willingness to listen carefully and ask questions

  o Do not interrupt.
  o Respond directly to the topic being discussed.

o It is better to not know and ask questions than to not know and seem confused.

- Perception that the interviewee is more interested in the organization and the requirements of the job than on the amount of paid time off, holiday schedule, and the pay scale of the job

   o Focus your answers and questions on the job and the organization. The topic of benefits has a time and place usually during the formal offer process.

- Knowledge of the organization, including sales figures, business areas, values, vision, and mission

   o Do your homework.
   o Your interest in the company states volumes about your commitment to the prospective job.

The manager's evaluation criteria does not change from the time the overall process commenced; to secure a team-focused resource that will perform the work required to close the gap that created the job opening. Realize that the hiring manager's reputation is, in part, in the hands of the employee hired. He or she now represents the manager in everything he or she does with his or her level of work performance. Once you are hired, you are institutionally transformed from a candidate to an employee and are considered an organizational investment. As an employee, you have agreed to an unwritten contract that requires you to commit to meeting and exceeding expectations at all levels of the organization at all times during your employment. Your new manager is, in turn, making a commitment to help you succeed, develop, and grow to your fullest potential. The expectation is that you will do the same for your manager and the organization. Your journey into the professional work environment expectation management, establishment, and fulfillment universe commences day one of your new job.

—•—

Diversify your experience, experience diversity, and orchestrate a better you.

—•—

CHAPTER 3

Experience Diversification

The most valued employees are those that can view situations from various perspectives and have developed the ability to arrive at solutions that are consistent with the vision, mission, and goals of their department and organization. Experience diversification can be described as the act of broadening your horizons. It is the means through which varying perspectives can be harnessed and cultured into seasoned, long-lasting business decisions.

Experience diversification is the end result of working within or closely with a variety of departments within the organization. Departments, groups, teams, or organizations are established by organizations to focus on the different areas of the business. These departments are experts tasked with specific responsibilities that are focused on a specific crucial area of the business. It is this focus that narrows the viewpoint of most departments. The effect of continued unchecked and narrow perspective norms inhibits viewpoint diversification which, in turn, inhibits the process of constructive teamwork and effective issue resolution. Organizations rely heavily on the norms that are inherently established when departments are granted authoritative decisions on a specific area of the business. Great organizations learn how to balance the focus of the various departments by facilitating cross-pollination among their employees. Choose to venture into the world of others, and you will see why and how they view challenges the way they do. Once you have lived in their business world, you can bring them into yours so that they too can experience the challenge from your vantage point. Only then will you both be able to arrive at a consensus that best supports the organization.

Understanding the role of the different departments within an organization is crucial in building your experience diversification. Most new-hire orientations are typically focused on three areas: organizational culture, processes, and your role and responsibilities within your department. Organizational culture addresses policies related to your employment such as ethical behavior, hours of work, dress code, holidays and time off, etc. Organizational processes addresses procedures related to your employment, such as timekeeping, help desk numbers, emergency evacuations, etc. Your departmental responsibilities discussion addresses manager expectations, job responsibilities, team introductions, etc. The missing link is typically a discussion about the other departments and how they interface with your department. Below is a symphony orchestra parable that will assist you in understanding why decisions are made and why, at times, these decisions appear to originate from left field. Similar to a business organization, a symphony orchestra is reliant on each musician, each instrument section, and the group as a whole to read the same sheet of music. Any deviation in understanding of this concept is a reflection of the conductor's ability to direct the orchestra and results in rogue notes that negatively affect the overall paying-customer experience. The quality of each note, of each cord, of each ensemble will determine the quality of the symphony. The quality of the symphony determines the number of opportunities it is offered to perform for the paying audience. Let's analyze the similarities between the company organizational departments and the symphony orchestra:

- Executive management is the symphony director for the company. Executives decide which of the available music scores, instrumentation, section, and combination of musicians best perform for the customer. The stock market's interest in the company is heavily based upon the effectiveness and reputation of the company's executive management. The major focus is to satisfy the vision and mission for the company.
- The business development and marketing departments are the behind-the-scenes promoters for the company. They perform market research, recommend business direction to executive management, and target specific business opportunities to pursue. These departments evaluate which music will be the most popular and generate the most sold-out shows for the symphony based on the talents and genre expertise of the musicians. Once identified, the business development and marketing department present executive management with a list of the selected scores,

music venues, and advertising strategies for consideration. These departments also market the talents of the symphony to its potential customers. The major focus is to bring in new work to the company. The show must go on all over the world.

- The operations department is the cast of musicians. They are tasked with producing the service or worked product promised to the customer by the business development department and the company. This department may encompass production, all services, manufacturing and engineering. Like any musician cast, the operations department is responsible for the quantity, quality, and timeliness of their masterpiece. The paying customer typically sees the product produced by the operations department firsthand as they sit in the audience and is either in amazement or in bewilderment. The major focus is production. The show must go on.

- The research and development department is the composer for the company. They are primarily tasked with innovation—to develop that which has not been developed before. This department experiments with the musical timing of and approach to the score and devises a new interpretation that is unique and marketable. This department finds new music in the old and develops innovative overtures. The service or product that is produced by the research and development department is forwarded to the various departments for a feasibility evaluation and production potential. The major focus is innovation. The show must go on in a new and better way.

- The finance department is the bookkeeper for and the financial conscience of the company and responsible for the administration and reporting of the company's finances, internally and externally. The symphony, as a company, must make financial decisions that can affect their ability to afford attire, hotel rooms, instruments, meals, travel, and musician salaries. There are times when trade-offs must be considered. The finance department provides company leadership with the financial advice required to make informed decisions. The major focus is money. The show must go on if the company can make a profit.

- The legal department is the behind-the-scenes protector and conscience of the company. They are primarily tasked with protecting the best interests of the company and its stockholders. The legal department handles contract and financial compensation disputes, insurance requirements, etc., for the symphony. The major focus is legal risk mitigation and risk reduction. The show must go on if the benefit outweighs the risk.

- The contracts department is the behind-the-scenes administrator of the company's contracts. They are primarily tasked with assuring the symphony's contract compliance with its customer, writing and interpreting contracts and contract approaches. The major focus is contract attainment and performance. The show must go on if everyone agrees on the terms and conditions.

- The human resources department is the people part of the company. In general, they are primary tasked with employee recruitment, attainment, moral, termination process, professional development and performance review process, benefits, wellness, and all other employee-based functions. The human resources department identifies, recruits, and hires the best musicians financially feasible for the symphony and offers musicians the opportunity to develop their talents beyond that of their current level. The major focus is employees and employee programs. The show must go on if the company has the talent.

- The communications department is the megaphone for the company. They are primarily tasked with all communications vehicles—internal and external—to the company. The communications department handles the media, the advertising, and, in part, the company image. Symphony performances, including venue and times, accomplishments, and promotional material and its communications, are administered by this department. The major focus is the proliferation of controlled information with the intent of creating and maintaining a positive company image. The show must go on, and the audience will know it.

- The quality or performance excellence department is the production check-and-balance entity for the company. They are primarily tasked with assuring that the company's products and services meet customer expectations. At show time, the symphony orchestra must hit every note precisely at the right time in order to produce the highest fidelity concert possible. A performance short of that helps the paying customer form a different kind of impression. The major focus is quality over quantity. The show must go on if it is a professional production.

- The environmental, health, and safety department is the protector of safe and healthful working conditions and a steward of the environment. They are primarily tasked with developing the processes that assure musicians do not develop injuries as the result of playing for an extended period of time, carrying their equipment, extended exposure to load sounds, etc. They are also tasked with developing processes that assure the symphony is a good steward of the environment by reducing its carbon footprint, by recycling, and by promoting energy and resource conservation. The show must go on if it is safe to do so, and the environment is not adversely impacted.

Departments are intertwined in a common cause designed to exceed customer expectations. Understanding the interrelationships between departments places you above the crowd in terms of business acumen and maturity. The key to developing experience diversification is to relentlessly seek to learn more about the inner mechanics of your company. Seek to understand what makes the business function and why. Take on additional responsibilities even though the new responsibilities may be outside of your comfort zone.

Good employees focus on becoming the experts in their chosen field of study. There is nothing wrong with this career path. Many professionals are content and successful within this comfort zone. *Great* employees focus on not only their chosen field of study but also on expanding their abilities and opportunities to grow with the company. Ability expansion is directly proportional to the willpower expended. You will find that many professionals are willing to help you understand their area of responsibilities. Accept these invitations because they will universally broaden your view of the business and offer the organization a much-valued employee.

Commit to rise above the situation; the climb is not that high. Glance beyond the horizon; seek to understand the other side. The right path is destined to emerge thereby guiding you to the right solution.

CHAPTER 4

Commitment and Resilience

In the business environment, commitment is the thread of success that sews your career and establishes an unwavering platform for resilience and professional longevity. Commitment is one of the core values that is unchangeable in changing times; it is partially the reason why professionals excel beyond that which others may find impossible, and it is, substantially, the reason why some employees advance at significantly faster rates than others within the organization. Commitment to your profession, team, company, and career, in itself, is not enough to succeed in the business environment. Add the element of resilience to your commitment with a heavy dose of respect, teambuilding, honor, and ethical behavior; and the results will be rewarding.

Young professionals inherently carry very few straws on their backs. Straws are those emotional detractors that we, as human beings, carry with us as reminders of the undesirable experiences we have encountered in our lifetime. The perception is that straws protect us from perceived or actual emotional harm. The natural tendency is for us to apply the same defense mechanism to the professional work environment. An example of this phenomenon can be demonstrated by evaluating the typical response when one employee has a negative encounter with another employee. One or both of the noted employees typically feel professionally offended in one form or another. This feeling, if left unchecked, places a straw or two on one or both of the employee's backs with a personal footnote that may include resentment toward each other. A subsequent negative encounter places another straw, possibly thicker, on their backs until, eventually, the structure holding these straws breaks, resulting in an out-of-control response to an otherwise minor situation. Out-of-control responses are frowned upon in the professional environment and will impact the organization's view of your ability to effectively handle issues. One of the keys to succeeding in your career is to not place straws on your back for long periods of time. To drop a couple of straws on the old back is human nature. To leave them there is unprofessional. Immediately address uncomfortable situations head-on and resolve to find solutions that best apply in consideration of all perspectives. Seeking the guidance of a good mentor is invaluable in these situations. Some seasoned professionals, unfortunately, have so many straws on their backs that they inadvertently allow these straws to guide their career and taint and limit their view of the real issues. Straws tend to cloud judgment, perception, objectivity, logical thought processes; and they erect filtered walls colored in depressive undertones and unhappiness. Straws erode away at the very foundational concepts of teamwork and productivity until the work afforded to that point is dissolved to a forgettable memory. Build instead a powerful structure of resilience that is capable of supporting and disposing of any straws placed on its frame. The secret to building a powerful and sustainable support structure is hidden within your ability to elevate above situations at levels higher than that presented by the moment. This ability introduces the powerful element of resilience as a foundational building block. Resilience is supported by the will to survive and the unrelenting belief that giving up is not an option regardless of the odds against you and the situation supporting those odds. Know that there is always a solution to every issue. Your resilience is the tool you possess that finds the brightness within the darkness and the strength within the weakness.

The backbone of resilience is perspective. The backbone of perspective is emotional stability. The backbone of emotional stability is confidence. The backbone of confidence is your support structure. The backbone of your support structure is the elemental needs that motivate us to breathe every day. Seek to view and rise above all situations to a level that affords you the opportunity to process thoughts, plan, and react professionally. This approach unveils the path that leads to a bountiful garden of possible solutions that are effective and ready for harvesting. Resilience counteracts your emotions and affords you the opportunity to better analyze and respond to any and all situations. Emotions have very little value in the business environment. As emotional beings, it is unnatural for us to understand situations purely on a factual basis, especially in the forefront of adversity. Good professionals control emotions, great professionals dominate them.

Switching from work life to home life and vice versa is a learned behavior that can be very difficult to manage effectively. Maintaining a separation between work issues and home life is highly recommended. The two are distinct and should be approached in different ways. The home life provides your support system for the challenges of your professional life; it helps in the administration, elimination, and control of your straws; it allows you to reboot and recharge and offers perspective and resilience to your thought processes. Realize that organizations do not consider your personal issues relevant to conducting business. Anything not relevant to conducting business is generally viewed as a distracter to the effectiveness of operations and the bottom line. Distractions do not play a role in most business plans and are therefore eliminated. Remaining professionally committed entails devoting your focus exclusively to the vision and mission of the organization. Remaining resilient necessitates progression to your uncompromising values, beliefs, and foundational structure. Effective domination of commitment and resiliency are desirable traits of a promotable professional in the eyes of an organization.

Perception is that entity which defies form and figure yet solidifies. It has no life yet lives in infamy. It has no physical strength yet has the power to build and to destroy. When harnessed appropriately, it purposefully protects all you have to offer: your reputation.

CHAPTER 5

Perception Is Reality

Perceptions, in the context of this book, are defined as those impulsive thoughts others experience when they think of you. When glancing at a window, most people simply see that view that is beyond the pane of glass. This view is only as wide and as tall as the window itself. Those attuned to a broader spectrum of stimuli and relentless pursuit of awareness glance at the same window and visualize much more. They see the view beyond the pane of glass in harmony with the reflection of all that is in the room, in front and behind them. The ability to visualize the different views from the same window that others have merely looked through defines the level of awareness an individual possess. A high level of awareness allows you to see what the organization thinks of your work and how the organization views or perceives your contributions to the business. In the professional environment, perception is more important than you think—it's everything.

Reputation stamps are noticeably invisible and legible marks that are unilaterally and indiscriminately awarded by employees to employees in organizations. Customers also award reputation stamps to companies in direct response to how they view the company meeting their expectations. The concept of perception determines the polarity, popularity, size, type, color, and texture of your reputation stamp. Everyone in business is attached to at least one reputation stamp that is visible across the organization. Very often, the reputation stamp is invisible to the adorned employee but blaringly visible to everyone else. They appear impulsively when others think of you, hear of you, and/or see you. The reputation stamp can be awarded by anyone in the organization and can read "professional" or something much less appealing. If a negative stamp is awarded, you will wear that reputation stamp until such time you prove yourself worthy enough to have it removed. You do not have a vote on removal rights. If a positive stamp is awarded, you will wear that stamp until such time you prove its message to be wrong in the eyes of the organization. Reputation stamps can help or hurt you professionally. Choose to manage your stamp carefully. The alternative is not advisable.

Most professionals understand that there is a difference between credibility and reputation. Credibility is established by the things you do to help others form an opinion of your actions. Reputation is established by the frequency at which you do the things you do. For example, meeting a commitment you made establishes favorable credibility. Predictably and consistently meeting all the commitments you make establishes a favorable reputation. Credibility is linked to single performances. Reputation is linked to the collection of performances and the trends anticipated based on those performances. Young professionals establish good credibility every day by exceeding the organization's expectations. Seasoned professionals establish reputations over the years by demonstrating reliable value to the organization. Losing your credibility destroys your reputation, always.

Reputation is perception, perception is reality, and both are indistinguishable relative to their role in professional advancement. The organization's perception of you significantly influences decisions that affect your career advancement. The organization's decision on whether to invest in you is highly dependent on how it perceives you will help the organization grow and prosper in the selected marketplace. Generally, help can only come from those whom are perceived can offer the assistance. For example, in the game of tug-of-war, two competitive teams pull a rope from opposite ends with the ultimate goal of overpowering their opponent to win. To win means to meet or surpass the objective. Successful teams hand select team members based on their ability, demonstrated or perceived, to significantly contribute in meeting or exceeding the objective. Team members require a set of playing rules, confidence, willingness, strength, endurance, and a team purpose to be successful. In business, the rope is the customers, the opposing teams are company employees, and the rules are the regulations and ethical standards the organizations elect to adapt or are required to adapt. As in the game of tug of war, organizations select only those employees it perceives will help the company beat their competitors. Characteristic traits are evaluated by management when looking at you as the person that will help pull the objective past the goal line. Your ability to project respectful confidence, willingness, expertise, and endurance helps convince the company to place you on their team.

Perceptions of weakness help convince the company to remove you from the team. Perceptions of weakness can materialize in many ways, often so subtle that you do not realize that the perception is in place. The following are examples of several of the perceptions you do not want your employer to believe are reality as they are viewed as weaknesses:

- Introducing your personal problems to the work environment and causing productivity distractions
- Suspected substance abuse resulting in financial risk to the organization and the causation of injuries or other undesired events
- A cluttered and disorganized office indicating your lack of organizational skills
- Office romance causing distractions and productivity issues among the other employees

Very often, professionals have a difficult time distinguishing the difference between the perceptions of being liked and being respected. Both relate to the kind of impressions you leave with other professionals. Both are related in that, if the conditions are right, one can lead to the other. There is, however, a major difference between the need to be liked and the need to be respected. Each focuses your attention on a very different path professionally.

The need to be liked is natural and demands a behavior that fosters external acceptance at any cost. Most people enjoy and actively seek the benefits of socializing and friendships. The need to be liked reinforces and validates acceptance and belonging. The excessive need to be liked in the professional environment can derail the chances for advancement and growth if left unchecked. The following are some of the effects than can materialize if the need to be liked controls your behavior:

- Your decision-making process is altered. Rather than formulating decisions that are based on the facts, you base your decisions on whether they will be viewed as conforming or popular. This approach leads to many reinforcing organizational dysfunctional behaviors, including group thinking and status quo operational expectations. Organizational dysfunctional behaviors, if not corrected, typically lead to loss of marketplace share and eventual self-destruction of the organization.

- The perception of organizational respect for your performance and abilities is impacted. In business, reputation and respect are everything. Nice guys are viewed as nice guys but incapable of compelling the organization to the next level. Competitive professional organizations desire employees with traits that exhibit aggressive pursuit of the objectives with a focus on innovation and the competitive edge and the wisdom to motivate others in the same direction. The ability to deliver is rewarded with the concept of professional respect.

The need to be respected is also natural and demands a behavior that is multifaceted—encompassing prioritization, expertise, and performance. Professional respect is mistakenly expected often and demanded as a matter of course rather than earned. In the simplest terms, respect can be aligned under two general categories: organizationally expected and professionally earned. Organizations are established with layers of management, each designed to work in unison in support of the vision and mission. Employees are generally expected to respect their employer and their management structure as a matter of unilateral course. A vice president walking into a meeting has a different effect on the population of the room than an entry-level employee entering the same room. This phenomenon is an example of an organizational expectation of respect. A highly regarded, highly productive, and highly touted employee speaking at a meeting has a different effect on the population than a similar speech offered by an employee who is simply liked but not respected. This phenomenon is an example of professionally earned respect.

There are many other situations that can affect how you are viewed and the perceptions that are derived from your actions, including that of your personal associations. In some cases, personal associations can prevent you from obtaining a job. This scenario is especially true if your job requires a security clearance. Personal associations can help or harm your career if they are comingled with your work environment. The classic example is that of a spouse, partner, or friend that you invite to a work-related social gathering. If your guest exhibits professional behavior during the event, the likelihood is high that you will be viewed in a similar light. If, however, your guest does not impress, the organization may question your ability to make the right choices.

Promotional advancement opportunities are available to the professional who has developed and implemented an effective campaign to build an impeccable reputation. Once established, your reputation is the perception and the tool organizations utilized to create the reality of success. Avoid the appearance of impropriety. Live on *integrity lane* and sleep well at night. Luck only manifests itself when the groundwork for achievement is nurtured by the desire to inspire greatness.

Tolerance is a tight rope supported by frequency and severity. It is defined by a band or otherwise that area between the acceptable and the taboo.

Chapter 6

Your Behavior, Your Appearance

Professionally venturing into the unacceptable is not advisable. Know that you represent the company. You are at work, whether you realize it or not, at company-sponsored events, and at friendly off-work gatherings with your colleagues, associates, competitors, business partners, and/or customers—former or current. If you are in the presence of one or more of this select group or if you are in attendance on behalf of the organization, you are at work, regardless of the time, day of the week, your location, or reason for your presence. The professional workplace behavior rules apply. How you behave, how you dress, how you communicate, how you socialize, and how you conduct yourself overall is discretely monitored and noted. The only safe haven from a professional workplace expectation is your personal life assuming you keep that separate from your professional life. There are, however, some personal behaviors that may affect your status at work, positively and negatively. Most of these behaviors revolve around behavior in the community and good citizenship. Personal problems with the law and behaviors that generate negative press are typically frowned upon in the professional environment. Personal commitment to volunteerism, community outreach, and commending media exposure are viewed positively. Work responsibilities that require a security clearance are highly sensitive to your personal activities outside of the work environment. Your personal associations with targeted groups could impact your ability to secure a classified job opportunity.

Understand that most organizations establish what is called *bands of tolerance*. A band of tolerance is defined as that space between what is acceptable and what is not acceptable to an organization in terms of behavior. It is in that space where organizations determine if employees are meeting expectations. Bands of tolerance are rarely discussed and vary in size greatly from manager to manager and from organization to organization. Employees who push to the edges of the bands of tolerance are viewed as purposefully pushing the organization's hot buttons without the possibility of disciplinary action. These employees are viewed as smart renegades interested only in their advancement and not in the team or the organization as a whole. Organizations have a way of handling employees, who choose to just barely stay out of trouble's grasp. Organizations limit professional development, promotional and career advancement opportunities to these employees. Bands of tolerance are a living organism. One day, the band may be as wide as an ocean exhibiting a very high tolerance for not meeting an expectation, and on another day, the band may be as narrow as a mountain creek, exhibiting a very low tolerance for not meeting the same expectation. The reason for this phenomenon is that organizations are comprised of people, and their behavior is sometimes not consistent from day-to-day. An example of this is if your boss simply jokes with you for arriving twenty minutes late one day last week yet issues you a disciplinary letter for arriving two minutes late one day this week. The width of a band of tolerance is dependent on many factors including the personality the manager, the financial stability of the company, the frequency of infractions, the perceived intent of the infractions, the employee's credibility, perceived intent, and established reputation. The following is an abbreviated list of actions to avoid in the professional working environment. These actions could derail a great career that consumed years to establish. These actions can also prevent a career from progressing. Reactions to these actions could be very subtle or could be very significant, depending on the situation, conditions, severity, and the organization's band of tolerance. Every professional must establish a hard line that must not be crossed. The list below will help you create substance for that line.

Most organizations typically have a *zero* band of tolerance for

- engaging in or promoting gossip in the work environment;
- dating your boss;
- romantic relationships within your department and sometimes within your organization, depending on size. Strained personal relationships will likely lead to noticeable strained professional relationships, which, in turn, lead to perceived risk for the

organization. Organizational risk means organization mitigation process initiation;

- engaging in physical or verbal altercations; never lose your cool;
- bringing your personal problems to work unless it is a life-changing event; your boss is your first line of defense;
- talking negatively about the organization, management, or colleagues;
- using organization resources for your personal gain, unless specifically allowed;
- charging time for work when you are not working for the organization;
- drinking alcohol or bringing or using illegal drugs in the workplace;
- reporting to work under the influence of alcohol or illegal drugs;
- bringing weapons to work unless authorized by the organization;
- lying, stealing, or condoning it in others;
- unethical behavior, including the falsification of records;
- behavior lacking in the principles of teamwork;
- consistently arriving late to work;
- consistently producing a poor quality work product;
- consistently missing commitments;
- not learning from mistakes;
- pointing the finger at others for your mistakes;
- text messaging, composing, or reading e-mails while in a meeting, unless specifically permitted;
- rudeness, including continuing to work while someone is talking to you; and
- attending a meeting without extending the courtesy of silencing your phone or pager.

Most organizations typically have a *narrow* band of tolerance for

- occasionally arriving late to work;
- occasionally producing a poor quality work product; and
- missing minor commitments.

Most organizations have a *wide* band of tolerance for

- justified absences;
- justified schedule slips;
- life-changing events, such as the birth of a child, loss of a spouse, purchase of a home, etc.

The key is to realize that these bands exist and to work toward remaining well within their center. Forget pushing the envelope on the band of tolerance. Your career success heavily depends on your ability to focus your attention in this regard.

Your choice of attire is a reflection of you and of your company. Your attire, personal hygiene, and grooming are important factors in the professional work environment. Your attire demonstrates commitment to yourself and others and facilitates certain elements of respect. Attire is generally an expression of self. Your personal taste in attire may or may not be suitable for the professional work environment. Very few organizations dictate exactly what their professional workforce should wear in terms of attire. Most organizations issue general guidelines and dress codes that describe the dress attire expectations. The professional environment, if not by policy then by expectation, does require a certain level of dress code of conduct. A professional must dress professionally in accordance with the expectations established by the employer. If you wish to determine the organization's standard for professional attire, notice how your organization's leadership dresses for the job. This is your clue as to the dress code expectations of an organization. Mimic this standard. Dress up to the position you seek.

Your behavior and your appearance speak volumes about your intentions, your career goals and aspirations, your commitment to the success of the team and the organization, and your general approach to your job. Allow your behavior to speak for you. Allow your appearance to open opportunistic doorways. Properly applied, both are fundamentally professional necessities that will consistently serve you well.

The concept of value is earned and perceived from a different set of eyes. Value is demonstrated, not articulated. Establish yourself as an indispensable and renewable commodity.

CHAPTER 7

Creating and Establishing Your Value

A commodity is an article of trade that can offset debt and offers net or perceived value to the bearer. Value or worth of a commodity is a perception in the eyes of an interested party that is based on trust. The concept of value, as a whole, is perceived from a different set of eyes. A fifty-dollar bill is only worth fifty dollars if the person receiving it believes it is worth fifty dollars. Entire international financial systems are built on the premise of trust. Instituting yourself as an invaluable commodity in the eyes of your employer places you on the fast track to advancement. Organizations tend to establish reward systems that are strictly based on employee results more often than they do reward systems that are based on employee efforts. Results are generally king of the corporate hill. Great efforts that do not yield great results are often viewed negatively and as poor utilization of precious resources. Uncompensated weekend work, long days and nights at the office, missed family events including vacations and personal sacrifices are lost to defeat if they fail to produce the expected results. Realize that you must perform to the organizational expectations or your value to the organization will be diminished. The stock markets hold organizations to the same set of rules, where investors reward stocks that increase in value and pay dividends, not stock portfolios that try hard and fail.

The importance of creating and establishing your value to the organization cannot be overstated. A purposeful approach that is designed to manage expectations is required. Remember that your value to the organization is only as significant as your organization perceives it to be—your personal evaluation of the value you offer the organization is irrelevant in the business environment. Value is demonstrated, not articulated. Create and establish your worth to the organization by utilizing the organization's expectations as the platform for your professional goals.

The homework in identifying the expectations pays dividends because it affords you the opportunity to develop an effective plan and set meaningful goals based on the expectations that matter at the end of the day. The business environment is highly metrics-driven and generally follows one rule: what is measured is what is accomplished. Measure your work performance progress of the organizational expectations, adjust process approach, and focus where required; and the likelihood is high that you will meet organizational goals and be viewed as a valuable employee by your employer. The following approaches help manifest and establish your value to the organization and enhance your job security:

- Accept challenges; raise your hand.
- Venture beyond your comfort zone.
- Be creative first, think of the possibilities second, consider the probability of success, and approach of the concept last. Think differently outside the confines of the group.
- Learn to recognize when help is needed and offer to help even when your schedule seems tight.
- Ask for help. It is okay to admit what you do not know.
- Focus on helping the team succeed.
- Recognize and admit when you are wrong, offer and accept apologies, and respect opposing views.
- Embrace diversity in its entirety with the presumption that the evaluation of challenges is simplified and facilitated more likely through the viewpoints of the many and less likely through the consideration of only one. Embracing diversity means embracing that which is different regardless of context. Good organizations welcome diversity as an essential part of business survival. Great organizations encourage and promote diversity as part of an imbedded cultural value. Your ability to accept diversity of thought, speech, approach, culture, race, and every other element of diversity defines the boundaries of your career advancement and success.

Job security is affected by many factors; some are within your control, and others are not within your control. Two important and closely linked factors affecting job security are the perception of value you create through your work performance and the level of organizational tolerance for your work performance at any given time. Figure 1 illustrates the effects that perceived value has on job security. On the left side of Figure 1, the organizational tolerance levels and perceived value to the organization range from low to high. On the bottom of Figure 1, employee performance level also ranges from low to high. Figure 1 is divided into four scenarios; each numbered from one through four. Figure 1 is further divided into the two broader states of the economy, booming and recessionary. The top section, scenarios one and four, characterizes a booming economy, a tolerant organization, and a time where there are more jobs than qualified applicants, in other words, an *employee's job market*. The bottom section, scenarios two and three, characterizes an economy in recession, an intolerant organization, and a time where there are more applicants than jobs available, in other words, an *employer's job market*. Scenario number one represents a situation where an employee is performing below average yet the organization is willing to tolerate this level of performance due to the prospering job market and the difficulties associated with attracting qualified applicants. In this scenario, the organization considers the employee's work performance to be of low value and will likely not invest in a long-term partnership. Job security is likely to be low in this case. Scenario number two is similar to scenario number one with a significant difference: the employee is now in an employer's market where qualified candidates are lined up for blocks hoping to take their job for less compensation. In this scenario, the likelihood is very high that the organization will seek to terminate the employee's employment at the first available opportunity. Job security and organizational tolerance are likely to be very low in this case. Scenario number three represents a situation where an employee is performing above average and the organization views the employee's work performance as very valuable; however, the economy is in a recessionary period. In this scenario, organizations generally protect high performing employees to an extent that is financially feasible. The employee, in this scenario, will experience a broader job security comfort zone than available in scenarios one and two. Understand that even a high-performer's job is at risk in an economy that is in recession. The organizational tolerance is lower for scenario number three because the state of the economy cannot support anything less than superior job performance. Scenario number four is similar to scenario number three with one major difference: the employee is now in an employee's market where employers are jousting for the best and the brightest candidates.

In this scenario, the likelihood is very high that the high-performing employee will be rewarded by the organization and the organization will invest heavily on the employee's career. The organizational tolerance is very high for minor mistakes in scenario four.

Take a step back; analyze Figure 1 and the story it foretells. The bottom line is that your job security is much higher when your performance exceeds the organization's expectations. While it is true that the economy may force layoffs regardless of employee performance, your chances of surviving the layoffs are higher if the organization truly values your ability to help it generate the revenue it needs to sustain the business model in critical economic times.

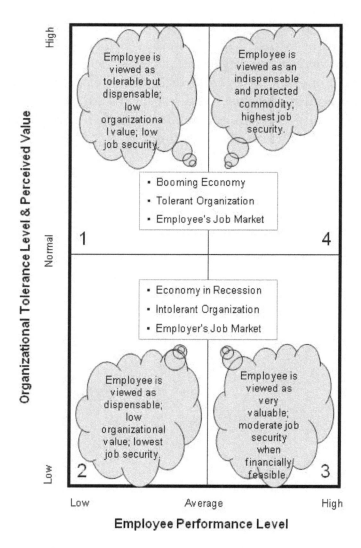

Figure 1 – The Effects of Perceived Value on Job Security

The benefits of becoming a high-performing, high-value employee in an organization is clear: enhanced job security and potential advancement. Recall that the concept of value is in the eyes of the organization. The possibility exists for you to be a high-performer and not be recognized for your efforts. This situation is usually the result of self-promotion efforts. The antidote to this situation is the art of self-advertisement. Learn the art of subtle self-advertisement and refrain from the practice of self-promotion. The most effective way to self-advertise is by performing your job to a level that exceeds your team's and the organization's expectations. The most effective way to promote your professional efforts is through team recognition of accomplishments. Self-promotion is an act of boasting without consideration for the team and/or the organization. Self-advertisement is a tactical act of self-promotion that utilizes your performance and the team concept to highlight your strengths and contributions. Self-advertisement follows the general premise that your high performance is only possible because of the team's success, and the team, inherently, promotes your accomplishments. Your team and you form a unit. The synergies created by facilitating self-advertisement through the team concept catapults your net worth to the organization in the eyes of the organization. For example, visualize a complex team project that has a very short schedule, tight budget, and the highest organizational and customer visibility possible. You are a member of a team whose sole purpose is to accomplish the work on behalf your company. You are not the team lead. Over the following weeks, you find yourself working longer hours, including weekends, to accomplish what you believe to be is the best project possible. You notice that your team member's efforts, although notable, are significantly less than your efforts. You continue to excel without reservation because you know the importance of a successful outcome to your organization. The team completed the complex project ahead of schedule, below budget, and exceeded the demanding customer's expectations. The organization subsequently receives accolades and additional work from the satisfied customer as a reward for the stellar performance on the first project. The project team is now a star in the eyes of management. Your team, realizing your significant contributions to this project, in turn, rewards your efforts within the organization by publically giving you the credit for the accomplishment. In this example, you advertised yourself through your unwavering professional performance while your team promoted your work on your behalf—thus illustrating the difference between self-advertisement and team promotion. Conversely, given the same scenario, if you, rather than your team, attempt to promote (self-promotion) your extraordinary efforts directly to the organization, you will inadvertently drive a wedge between you and your teammates. The latter is a simplified example of how self-promotion encourages an undesirable perception—not being a team player. The former is a simplified example of how self-advertisement encourages a desirable perception—being a team player. Both scenarios are examples of perception management; one yielding better results than the other.

Your approach to creating and establishing your value in the eyes of the organization can help or hinder the acceptance of your work product. An example of this is the acceptance or rejection of your ideas. The best ideas in the world are nonexistent if the world is not cognizant of their presence. The best ideas in the world tend to remain in obscurity if they are presented in a way that undermine the organization; hence, the importance of understanding the consequences of selecting self-advertisement or self-promotion approaches. Ideas presented appropriately are considered and appreciated by all in organizations. There are other opportunities besides self-advertisement to demonstrate your value to the organization. The performance review process, activity reports, and successful completion of tasking are examples that help you advise the organization of your net worth.

Your health is viewed as a value factor, a commodity type, in most organizations. Great employee health translates to a lower overall risk for the organization. The probability of your career advancement is higher if the organization can forecast a return on their investment in you. For example, the likelihood is very high that an organization will invest thousands of training and promotional dollars on an employee that is fit for duty. An organization is likely to invest in an employee whose health is perceived to be a positive performance-factor influence. Some professions require a certain level of physical fitness as part of the job qualification criterion. Maintain a healthy lifestyle, and you will create the perception of added value to your organization.

Establish yourself as an indispensible commodity by focusing on delivering value in the eyes of your employer. Value is delivered when predictable, measurable, and consistent results are delivered dependably. Expectations that your boss will remember your accomplishments are unrealistic. It is your responsibility to keep track of your accomplishments and to help your boss build a center stage for each one. To be noticed by affirmation introduces the concept of obscure intent. To be noticed by association among top talent introduces the concept of viable opportunity.

The final step in the process of creating and establishing your value to the organization is to understand the concept of *total compensation* and how it could impact your employer's perception of the value you offer to the organization. Total compensation is that amount which your employer views as its financial obligation for your services and may include the following elements:

- Financial Compensation

  o Base Pay (this is how much you agreed to work for and is typically the amount you see before taxes on your paycheck)
  o Performance Sharing (this is how much of the annual profit your employer shares with you)
  o Stocks (this is how much of the actual company ownership your employer awards you)

- Retirement Compensation

  o Social Security (you pay half; your employer pays half)
  o Retirement Plan (you contribute; your employer may contribute)

- Health and Welfare Compensation

  o Medical, Dental, and Vision Insurance (you contribute; your employer contributes)
  o Life and Disability Insurance (you contribute; your employer contributes)
  o Workers' Compensation Insurance (this insurance covers your medical costs and some of your paycheck if you are injured at work; your employer pays this cost)
  o Paid-Time-Off Including Vacations and Holidays (you earn this; your employer pays the bill)

- Professional Development Investment

    o   Mentoring (this is the cost associated with the time and effort a mentor devotes to you to help you succeed; your employer pays for this expense)
    o   Educational Assistance (this is the cost associated with seeking a degree or an advance degree; you contribute; your employer contributes)
    o   Internal Training (this is the cost associated with you taking on-the-job training or formal in-house training classes; your employer pays for this expense)
    o   External Training (this is the cost associated with you taking off-the-job training or formal third-party training classes; your employer pays for this expense)

- Non-tangible Expenditures

    o   Productivity Loses (these are the costs associated with you not performing to your highest potential)
    o   Errors and Omissions (these are the costs associated with your mistakes; your employer pays for this expense)
    o   Morale Event (this is the cost associated with employee holiday, event, and milestone celebrations; your employer pays for this expense)

This list could be longer or shorter and is contingent upon your position within the organization and the organization's compensation programs. The direct cost of your services to your employer can be as low as one-hundred and forty percent to as high as two-hundred percent of your salary or higher. Your paycheck is only the beginning from an organization's financial perspective. The key take-away here is to understand that your employer evaluates your contributions, in part, against the total compensation package it offers for your services. If the organization views the value of your contributions as exceeding the value of your total compensation, then you are viewed as a valuable resource. Valuable resources are typically placed on the bottom of the list during lay-offs and employment retention decisions. Your understanding of the total compensation concept offers you another important tool in the approach to establishing and creating value in the eyes of the organization.

More and more organizations are including *economic stress clauses* in their hiring documentation, contracts, and in organized labor agreements. In simple terms, economic stress clauses are agreements that allow employers to change or reduce the level of total compensation an employee or group of employees receive based on the financial outlook of the organization. Economic stress clauses are lifelines for organizations because they offer the flexibility to cut costs during critical periods of financial vulnerability. Employees are financially affected by the implementation of these clauses through wage, benefit, and other compensation reductions. The alternative to economic stress clauses in employment contracts could include extensive layoffs, facility closures, and ultimately, bankruptcy. These clauses are a direct product of the tough economic times generally experienced during recessions. Other economic stress factors that can cause the introduction and implementation of economic stress clauses in organizations include loss of market share to competitors, bad investments, and undesirable factors related to reputation, customer, and investor confidence. Your employer may require you to sign an employment agreement containing economic stress clauses. When you sign the agreement, you have tied your financial success with the financial success of the organization. Your ability to create and establish a high organizational value for yourself will reduce the risk of economic stress clause enforcement during your employment. The organization will likely weigh the risk of you seeking and finding other employment against the risk of accepting the costs associated with not implementing the economic stress clauses. The organization's risk-based decision is simpler when you are a valued employee.

Identify expectations; learn what is measured; focus on delivering positive and actionable results; allow your performance to speak for you; keep track of accomplishments; understand the concept of total compensation and the pressures that organizations are under to cut costs especially during economically stressful times. Your willingness and ability to undertake the quest for solutions to these challenges will establish you as an invaluable resource to the organization. Employers require only one of two justifications for your employment status: a justification to keep you on the payroll or a justification to let you go. Economic stress factors aside, the employer will choose the justification that undoubtedly reflects your value to the organization. Establish yourself as an indispensible and renewable commodity. Offer your organization the justification they require to support you in your career.

Your communications are everlasting and memorable. Once departed, forever remembered.

CHAPTER 8

Communication Strategies

How, when, where, and how much you choose to communicate is a significant factor in the advancement of your career. Your words and actions—written, verbal, or implied—last forever in organizations. They are cemented in place once you have set them free. Commitments are carried on the framework of communications vehicles. What and how you communicate exposes the person you are, your emotional state and stability, and your true biases. Discretion in communications is a highly sought-after quality in prospective leaders. Mastering this art is a key to securing a bright and successful future. Communications establish commitments. Commitments establish expectations. Expectations establish performance criterion. Performance criterion establishes priorities. Priorities establish what is important to the organization. You will be held accountable for your professional communications, good or bad. What you say is as important as how and when you say it. In business, a "loose cannon" is an employee who is perceived to defy authority and communicates out of turn and inappropriately across various levels of the organization. One of the undesirable characteristics of the "loose cannon" is the inability or unwillingness to communicate in accordance with the organization's expectations. Avoid this forehead stamp. Establish communication protocol with your boss and follow the guidance offered. Your boss will provide you with the communication licenses you need in order to perform your work effectively. The following lessons learned will enhance the likelihood of success in all of your professional communications:

- No surprises for your boss. Your boss must know all. Ask your boss for input when in doubt. Good bosses expect bad news once in a while. Great bosses encourage the reporting of it without retribution. Most great bosses expect to learn of bad news from their team (you) and not from the organizational grapevine.

- The salient factor is how the other party received your communication and not how you intended to deliver the message. Your intentions pale in comparison.
- Adapt the twenty-four hour rule of written communications. This rule helps you craft an effective response to communications that triggers negative emotions twenty-four hours after the fact; whenever the situation allows. Proceed with writing your impulsive response immediately but avoid transmission until you have had a chance to consider the other possible approaches. Writing an impulsive response on day one helps you work through your emotions. Read your response on day two. The short waiting period will undoubtedly change the tone and approach of your communication. Time is an invaluable advisor when you use it appropriately.
- Communications can be sent through the traditional means such as verbal, written, or electronic. Messages can also be sent through non-intentional methods, such as facial and body expressions, behavior, the silent treatment, etc. Be aware that all communications in the work environment are subject to evaluation and critique.
- You must anticipate and consider potential outcomes of your communications before you transmit.
- Spell and grammar check all written communications.
- Articulate your words.
- Speak intelligently and with confidence.
- Expand your vocabulary. Vocabulary size matters.

Open meetings offer a different dynamic relative to communications. An open meeting occurs when three or more professionals meet to discuss a work-related topic. People are more sensitive to the perception of reputation, respect, and team dynamics in open meetings. Open meetings are not the generally accepted forums to discuss issues related to individuals. Be mindful of what you communicate in open meetings. The goal is to assure your communication does not publically and negatively affect the reputation of another individual or diminishes the benefits of teamwork. Effective communications is a foundational requirement in the professional work environment.

Licenses all have one thing in common: they expire. Renewal is at the discretion of the grantor.

CHAPTER 9

Understanding Licenses

In business, professional employees are issued unwritten, untold, unexplained freedoms or licenses that are based on expectations of your position within the organization and the organization's culture. There are many variations of licenses granted by organizations, bosses, and colleagues. All have one trait in common: they expire. One sure way to identify license status is in the way others react to your actions. Positive reactions indicate that all is well; your licenses are valid. Negative reactions indicate that one or more licenses were either never granted or that they expired. Examples: You typically have an inferred license to stop anyone within your organization to introduce yourself and converse in detail about your job and their job. You typically do not have a license to engage in the same topic of conversation at a professional development conference with a competitor's employee. You normally have a license to speak about business issues directly to your boss's management as long as your boss is aware of the topic of discussion and agrees to the discussion; this is called protocol. An example of a license that is not granted is when your boss is not aware that these conversations are occurring. His or her reaction to you discussing business issues with upper management will provide you with an indication that a license was never granted to you for this action.

The following is a short list of examples of licenses that are typically issued to young professionals. You are allowed and expected to

- make mistakes (expiration occurs when you do not learn from your mistakes);
- question established approaches or processes (expiration occurs when you do not provide viable alternative solutions);

- make suggestions that are viewed as radical (expiration occurs when you do not accept the organization's decision on your recommendations); and
- be innovative and creative (expiration occurs when your ideas are not in-line with the organization's vision and mission).

Innovative and creative organizations tend to have greater flexibility when it comes to allowances for mistakes. All organizations expect you to learn from your mistakes and not repeat their occurrence. The organization's financial posture in the marketplace and its willingness to push the envelope also has an effect as to the types and frequency of licenses it issues to its employees. Realize that licenses can be granted and taken away without your knowledge. Indicators or clues are provided in the way the organization, your boss, and your colleagues react to you and your approach to your work. The fertile ground is provided to you at the start of your new job. The organization's tolerance for your actions and depth of licensure depends upon the types of seeds you plant, nurture, and harvest.

Most people favor a tendency to forget the issue and an even greater tendency to never forget your approach.

CHAPTER 10

Diplomacy and Protocol

Diplomacy is the vehicle through which all messages are delivered. The kind of message—good, bad, or indifferent—is insignificant when compared to the method selected to deliver the end result. Protocol is the set of rules, either written or inferred, by which organizations execute diplomacy. The concept of diplomacy encapsulates protocol, approach, timing and appropriateness, status of granted licenses, and communications history and emotional state of both the communicator and the recipient. Understand that every situation requires some level of diplomacy to reach a mutually acceptable solution. Your willingness to follow established protocol is a preferred character trait that management appreciates in the professional environment. The following protocol guidance recommends several actions that promote diplomacy and establishes acceptable behavior in the eyes of leadership:

- Never complain to an individual's boss about anything negative without advising the subject individual first. Always provide the opportunity for the other party to explain their position or correct the issue. On the occasion that the issue remains unfulfilled without a potential possible resolution, it is appropriate to advise the other party that you will be contacting their boss and/or escalating the issue to upper management for resolution. Warning: be advised that your management notices how many issues you bring to the table without resolution. The general expectation is that you only bring solutions to the table and not unsolved issues. Your ability to solve issues at your level is monitored and evaluated during promotional opportunities.

- Determine all possible stakeholders or parties that may be impacted by your work. Engage them as part of your team. Inclusion promotes diplomacy.
- Never communicate with your boss's boss or higher without your boss's blessing. Be mindful that your communications to the senior management may not be derived from the same data sets that are available to your boss.
- If your organization is subordinate to another organization, never communicate with the parent organization without having a license to do so. The same is true with all communications outside your organization. Ensure that you have the authority and permission to communicate with external entities. Your boss is the only person that can grant you these licenses.
- Never engage in active job-hunting activities within your organization without your boss's knowledge. Your boss can either help you or reduce your chances of obtaining the job you seek. Warning: you run the risk of sending an inadvertent message to your boss when you advise him or her of your intentions to apply for another job within the organization if you do not handle the communication properly. Your boss can view you as temporary help and may stop his or her investment in you. The correct approach is to have frank discussions with your boss about your career goals and aspirations and ask him or her for their help in reaching their fulfillment. In short, include your boss in your career development plans, and the probability is higher that he or she will help you reach your goal.

Know that office politics is an integral part of the professional environment. Master this concept, and your career aspirations will be facilitated. Ignore diplomacy and protocol and the likelihood is high that your career will be short-lived.

Expect more of yourself than you normally do of others. Expect no more of others than you normally do of yourself. Your perception of yourself does not count nearly as much as their perception of you.

CHAPTER 11

Build Trust, Build a Good Reputation, Build Alliances

Membership into a workplace team requires an investment from both you and the team. The "Members Only Pass" can only be obtained through the slow process of trust development and nurturing. A manager can assign you to a team by his or her authority, but the true invite and acceptance only comes from the team as everyone begins working toward a common goal. The best teams are formed through trust and alliances. These alliances can only be built once trust is established, the element of individual competition is subdued, and the perception of teamwork is the only possible option.

Recall that reputation is one of those tangible, intangible, nonphysical entities that is redefined and evaluated every day. It is, at the end of the day, the only larger-than-life commodity you have to offer, which provides your employer and others a reliable forecast of your performance. Reputation is also a foundational building block for establishing trust. Everyone in the working environment has an input in defining your reputation from the lowest level employees to senior management; therefore, everyone in the work environment has a say into whether you can be trusted or not with organizational resources, sensitive information, and performance to work requirements. Many employees formulate the mistake of believing that only their team and management have a vote into the evolvement of their reputation. The fact is that many reputations are blemished and, conversely, improved by the person least expected. There are many examples where the lowest-ranking person in an organization has negatively affected the promotional chances of an individual that is not in their department. This scenario typically manifests itself in casual conversations in the most informal of settings. The opposite is also true. Situations have occurred where a contractor's employee positively influenced the decision of a senior manager to promote an individual based on the contractor employee's stellar testimonial of the courteous and professional treatment she receives during every visit. Building trust builds a reputation. Building a good reputation builds alliances. Building alliances simplifies the task of creating the perception of value. The professional impact one unexpected person can have on another's career is a phenomenon that is rarely recognized and understood. The antidotes to this phenomenon are to treat everyone equally and with respect and integrity, expect more of yourself than you do of others, admit and learn from your mistakes, and apply the lessons learned strategically. Treat *everyone* as if they are important because they are; your treatment of them is the first step to building trust.

Customers are not a bother; their demands are the only reason for your job. Customers must be treated with respect and sense of importance regardless of their requests.

Chapter 12

The Customers

Know your customers. They are everyone you come in contact with at work, who depends on or expects a work product or service from you. Anyone initiating a request or has established an expectation is a customer. Note that there are internal customers and external customers. Both require special handling.

Internal customers work toward a common goal in support of the external customer. They share a common vision through the eyes of the organization. Effective internal customer relations translate to effective external customer relations. Great organizations spend significant resources to ensure that employees share a common cause through the establishment and communication of expectations and results-based processes. Your approach to your coworker's jobs influences, positively or negatively, the performance of the overall organization. This is one of the main reasons why organizations insist on teamwork-based approaches and only recruit prospective employees that exhibit this trait.

Most organizations depend on external customers for survival. External customers depend on other organizations to perform work they cannot accomplish themselves. Depletion or extinction of the external customer base inevitably forces the same fate for an organization. In that way, organizations and customers are bound in an eternal relationship of dependent survival. External customers are the reason you are or will be employed, period. How external customers are treated—how their issues are resolved, how well your organization meets its commitments to them, how well your organization represents them, how predictable and reliable your organization performs—determines if they will continue to conduct business with your organization or if they will find another one of several other organizations to support their initiatives.

Your employer considers its customers a privilege, not a hindrance. Customers are not a bother; they are the reason for your job. The best customer your organization has is the one it is serving *today*. This customer provides the critical financial resources necessary for survival and sustainment in the ultracompetitive business world. In representing your organization, your actions directly impact the external customer's view of your organization. You have a major responsibility in this regard. Your representation can come in a variety of ways from direct contact to indirect contact. Internal quality of your service and product are examples of indirect contacts with the customer. It does not matter if you are the employee responsible for maintaining the facility or designing a new product or providing an IT service. The fact remains that all employees in an organization affect the customer's view of the organization through their work product performance. Every employee matters.

There is no greater foundational requirement for an organization than to exceed its customer's expectations. By virtue of this concept, there is no greater foundational requirement for an employee than to exceed its organization's expectations. Performance that is forged within an alternative concept is lacking in the realities of the business environment. To that end, the very reason for your employment is, in fact, etched in the successful efforts of your coworkers and their passion in satisfying the needs of the external customer. Thank them. You are intertwined as a team and in competition with the world for the external customer's business and your jobs.

Listen to what others are telling you; it really is important, not sometimes, but always.

CHAPTER 13

Dominating Difficult Situations

Everyone, no matter how skilled they are in people skills, will encounter difficult situations where professional and possibly personal verbal engagements are experienced. These situations could manifest themselves through the rumor mill, in open meetings, or during one-on-one encounters. Most situations all have at least one commonality: viewpoint divergence. How each involved party perceives an issue determines the intensity of the situation. How you handle the disparity in viewpoint will determine the other party's perception of you as a professional. Ultimately, recall that perceptions become the forefront of reality. The following streamlined process helps elevate you above the situation and helps guide others into viewing you as a team player and a true professional:

- Listen first. Listen carefully. Take notes. Remove emotions and biases as much as practical. Rise above the event, and think about the big picture. Project an image of concern over the situation and the willingness to resolve the issue. Behave as if a room full of upper management were closely listening to and watching your reaction.
- Be very aware of your surroundings. Know that some discussions are best conducted in private. Always avoid discussing difficult situations in public. Discussions in person are the best approach. Understandably, this option is not always available. The next best communication approaches in order of preference are noted below:

    o   Video broadcast
    o   Telephone call

- o Electronic format (e-mails survive a lifetime)
- o Follow up all electronic communications with an in-person discussion or, alternatively, with a telephone call.

- Step into the shoes of the other party. Try to evaluate the situation from their point of view.
- Ascertain the drivers behind emotional outbursts and neutralize them by summarizing what you heard in a professional and caring manner.
- Respond only when the other party has completed the venting process. Your time to speak is when the other party acknowledges your summary to be accurate.
- If you are wrong, admit it immediately. Take responsibility for your actions. Honestly thank the other party for bringing the issue to your attention. Take corrective action and follow up with the other party to assure the situation is defused.
- If you feel your point of view is correct after hearing the other side of the story, attempt to bring the other party into the way you view the situation and explain your position. State your case. Repeated interruptions from the other party indicate that they are not listening. The best approach is to politely table the discussion for a time when cooler minds will prevail.
- Always remain professional, stick to the facts, be accurate in your statements, treat the other party with respect, and elevate to your boss any issues you feel are too large or complex for you to handle. You will learn how to handle most situations with experience.
- Always advise the other party of your intended actions after the discussion. They should never be surprised of your actions or reactions.

Situations do arise that prove to be very challenging for you to handle by yourself. Recognize these situations and seek assistance from your management. Great organizations have outlet vehicles for their employees that offer help and guidance on a variety of issues. Acquaint yourself with these services and use them as appropriate. The ability to handle difficult situations is a trait that organizations value and reward in high potential employees.

You are only as good as your boss says you are. Your performance is your boss's performance in the eyes of the organization.

High-maintenance employees are dispensable. Low-maintenance employees are indispensable.

CHAPTER 14

Your Boss

Everyone has a boss, even the boss. Many careers have ended or were subdued simply due to the relationship between the employee and the employee's boss. Many careers have blossomed for the same reason. This chapter is the most important chapter in the book. Building a strong and healthy relationship with your boss forms an indelible partnership. This partnership will earn you licenses and protections that you would not otherwise be awarded or provided. It is important to understand that it is your responsibility to foster a healthy partnership with your boss. After all, you are hired on the basis that you promised to offer your boss the services he or she needs to help the organization succeed. Everyone is prone to making mistakes, the frequency and severity of which is higher during the early years of a professional career. A partnership with your boss offers you with the opportunity to transform those mistakes into invaluable lessons learned with minimal collateral damage to your reputation and your career with the organization. True lessons learned encourage positive behavior enhancement. Positive behavior enhancement evolves into potential in the eyes of the organization. Potential creates the perception of value. The perception of value significantly increases the probability of career advancement.

Young professionals have the opportunity to start anew. Your perspective on your boss's role can either establish a mutually beneficial relationship or cultivate a short-lived tenure in the organization. Fortify the following mind-sets in a solid foundation as these are among the most important attributes of an employee and boss relationship:

- Your boss is ultimately expected to answer for your actions, mistakes, and triumphs. Your performance is the boss's performance in the eyes of upper management. Your boss's reactions to situations are almost always as a result of this fact.

- Your boss is the most important person in the organization who can help you grow and expand your career.
- Your boss is the first member of your team and alliance.
- Your boss can rescue you from certain professional peril. You cannot do it on your own.
- The only way you will be viewed as valuable to the organization is if your boss is viewed as valuable to the organization.
- Always take the loaded and oversized backpack off your bosses' back and place it on yours. Walk it up the rocky, rain-slicked mountain for him or her. Leave the complaints back at the cabin by the fireplace. Present solutions to your boss, not unmitigated problems. Always work toward making your boss look good.
- Make your boss's job easy even if your job is tough.
- Give your boss credit for your accomplishments and achievements. Your boss's accomplishments reflect on you and the rest of the team.
- Your boss assigns work to you based on the needs of the organization. Sometimes the reasons are not obvious. Trust your boss's judgment.
- Your boss's priorities are your priorities. Your boss establishes your priorities.
- Respect your boss's position within the organization.
- Your boss may not know how to perform your job as well as you. That is why you were hired.
- Work the same number of hours per day your boss works when practical. Arrive to work early, leave work late. Arriving later and leaving earlier than your boss is not advisable.

Warning: Priorities are in the eyes of the beholder. You must assure that your boss is in-line with your perception of the true priorities. You will not be able to please everyone, but you must please your boss. Evaluate your workload, work with your boss to determine schedules for completion, make the commitments, and perform. Employees find themselves under disciplinary action most often due to perception discrepancies related to priorities. You are expected to speak up if you cannot meet a deadline or if there is a newly introduced deadline that conflicts with previous direction.

Part of your boss's job is to help you help the organization by assigning work within your capabilities and within your productivity output rate. Part of your boss's job is to also challenge you beyond your limits as this is the only way to determine your potential.

You have two major jobs in your role as an employee. The first job is to perform your job to the best of your ability. The second job is to help your boss perform his or her job better. Provide your boss with a reason to help you succeed and you will. The alternative is also true.

Your success is directly tied to your boss's success. Performing well and offering credit for your work to your boss will pay dividends in the short and long run. Alternatively, the appropriate time to seek other employment is when the relationship between your boss and you is perceived to be irreconcilable. Years of experience have demonstrated that tactful approaches bring out the best in both the boss and the employee. Focus on the mission, the boss's mission, and the weekends will be much more enjoyable.

A performance review is your opportunity to showcase your accomplishments. A performance development plan is your assurance that your organization is willing to invest in your future.

CHAPTER 15

Performance Reviews and Performance Development Plans: The Inner Workings

In academic life, tests are administered to periodically demonstrate proficiency in each class topic where a letter grade of C or D is typically considered passing, the learning institution offers time to prepare and the subject of the exam is generally known in advance. In the business world, tests are administered every day without the option of failure. Expectations and professional evaluations are the business jargon for examinations, where the only acceptable outcome of an exam is an A if you are to succeed. At times, even an A performance in the work environment is not enough to stand out among other high performing employees. The business environment oftentimes does not offer the luxury to prepare for daily professional evaluations nor does it offer advance notifications of an exam. You must be on your game every day. Failure to meet a professional expectation could mean your job and possibly your career.

Great organizations have an effective system that helps their employees develop and grow through the process of expectation establishment and measurement. Performance reviews are often times viewed as a manager's chance to talk to the employee about the gaps in performance. This is true if the organization culture has not invested in establishing effective performance review programs, including training for employees and managers. In reality, the performance review is an opportunity for the employee to showcase accomplishments and to have meaningful discussions with the manager about expectations, professional development, and potential career paths. The performance review process begins with you doing your homework. Know where you are, where you want to go, and your approach to reaching your career goals and the organizational goals. Your boss is the organization's facilitator tasked with ensuring that you have a solid performance review and development plan in place. A good organization typically measures your boss's success, in part, on the level of your success. This approach establishes a common ground based on teamwork. A performance development plan is a management tool that lays out an effective path for you and your boss to follow in order to reach your developmental goals. Performance development plans typically identify additional educational and professional opportunities. Performance reviews and performance plans are sometimes present on one document.

Organizations typically follow two rules of thumb relative to performance: (1) what is measured is what is important to the organization and (2) what is important to the organization is undoubtedly noticed. High performance to goals is important to organizations and is often rewarded with job security and/or financial incentives for the employee. Most performance reviews are based on your boss's perception of how you met the established professional goals. Professional goals are those goals that help the business succeed or business goals. Career goals are those personal goals that help your career. Know that your boss sets his or her own professional goals based on the business goals established by upper management. Your professional goals are based on your boss's professional goals. Understand that business goals are flowed down to all levels of the organization from top to bottom. Your professional goals must be in-line with your organization's goals and your career goals. Assist your boss in identifying your professional and career goals. Disparities in this approach create perceived performance irregularities subject to uncomfortable discussions and downgrades in your performance evaluation.

The following actions are recommended for employees starting a new position:

1. Know the job or know the requirements of the position.
2. Know your bosses' expectations (professional goals) for your performance.

    a. Understand the work schedule including work hours and work location(s).
    b. Relative to your job, specifically know the performance expectations and the actions required to exceed those

expectations; be specific. Establish meaningful, attainable, and measurable goals that are aligned with your boss's goals. Tie your boss down to the details and avoid subjective performance expectations. A detailed expectation may read, "Submit activity report at the end of every fiscal month. The report shall contain, at a minimum, customer contacts, major milestone accomplishments, and planned new activities for the next reporting period." A subjective performance expectation may read, "Submit a monthly activity report." Details included in performance expectations benefit the employee and the manager.

   c. Identify your boss's communication protocols. Ascertain the acceptable points of contact for your day-to-day communications.

   d. Discuss the process for handling issues when they come up.

   e. One note on pet peeves: identify the hot buttons early; ask your boss. Good bosses recognize their pet peeves; great bosses communicate them to their employees.

3. Document your understanding of the performance discussions with your boss and submit to him/her for revision/approval. This is the plan that will measure your performance and will help the organization determine if you are a high-potential employee. Changes to expectations should also be documented as the performance evaluation process is a living document.

4. Advise your boss of your career goals. Discuss and document a performance development plan that is in-line with your career goals. Remember that your career goals must be in-line with the organization's and your department's goals. A goal-alignment disparity could cause disappointments on both sides. An intentional misalignment with your department's goals is effectively advising your boss that you are looking to leave the department.

5. Work toward exceeding expectations and track your performance to the performance review and performance development plan.

6. Communicate with your boss often to assure that you are meeting and exceeding expectations. This approach will identify perception issues early and will allow time to change direction if required.

7. Your performance is your boss's performance. Take the initiative to perform to a level that reflects well on your boss and your team. Volumes are spoken if your boss or your team takes credit for your work.

8. On the occasion that either your boss forgets or the workload prohibits a performance review and/or a performance development discussion, tactfully set up a meeting with your boss as a reminder.

Remember, a performance review is your opportunity to ascertain your boss's expectations, to assess your perceived value to the organization, and to showcase your talent and accomplishments. A performance development plan is your assurance that your organization is willing to invest in your future. Both are very important and required to achieve success in the professional working environment. Both can be positive experiences if you choose to view and approach the process appropriately. Tactfully insist on these discussions. Your career path depends on their occurrence. You can guide the outcome of these discussions toward your objectives as long as your objectives are complementary to the organizational vision and mission. Grasp the opportunity convincingly.

Networks are lifelines in the business environment; size does matter a lot.

CHAPTER 16

Personal Professional Development, Networks

The only person responsible for your professional development is yourself. This responsibility cannot be delegated away. Professionals must forge a path paved with the desire to continuously improve. Relentless pursuit of knowledge is a minimum requirement for success.

The funding that is available for your professional development greatly depends upon the organization's financial standing and forecasted outlook. Most good organizations realize that their competitive edge is only as sharp as their employees. These organizations also realize that very few investments return the value that is offered by knowledgeable, up-to-date professional labor. The marketplace competition and the corporate desire to gain more of the market share helps you sell the concept of attending professional conferences, specific target area courses, advanced degrees, and seeking professional certifications. Professional development can also come in the form of supporting other departments and taking advantage of in-house learning opportunities. Your interest and pursuit of professional development opportunities advises the organization that you are adaptable and welcome change, a trait highly desired in today's management teams.

Great organizations have programs that develop young talent into world-class leaders. These programs are generally available to those who are willing to work in a variety of jobs over a several years at most, if not in all the organizations within the organization. Fast-track leadership development programs are carefully tailored toward developing future leaders within the organization and offer the opportunity to establish a far-reaching and effective professional network. Large professional networks facilitate the ability to derive solutions to challenges, they open doors of opportunity, and offer two of the major benefits of the program—experience diversification and professional exposure. Experience diversification is described in the next chapter. In short, the wider your viewpoint of the inner workings of the organization, the higher the probability of success for your and the organization. Professional exposure relates to the opportunities available to you as a contributor to the success of the business. Get positively noticed by as many people as possible, and you will be considered when a great opportunity is available. Experience diversification is a form of preparation. Professional exposure is a form of opportunity generation or fabrication. Fast track leadership development programs are the expedited delivery vehicle for both.

Organizations typically invest significant resources in the participants and are therefore very selective. The keys to securing a spot in a leadership development program are to express an interest, create the perception that you are worthy of the investment, and demonstrate that you have the work ethic to see the program through its completion.

Effective professional development plans include the resources for securing professional certifications. Seek to engage and participate in professional societies, certify through their testing process, and gain access to their networks. Professional certifications are a gateway toward respect when expressing opinions or providing solutions to complex issues. The professional work environment reacts differently and positively to those who they perceive posses the professional qualifications and certifications. Additional opportunities are available to those who make the effort and take the time to obtain the recognition of third-party certification organizations.

Networking is another vehicle that supports professional development and many other areas of your career. The importance of establishing a stable matrix of networks cannot be overstated. Many great books are already written on how to establish effective networks. Realize that your development, your career opportunities, and the realization of your goals are all standing on the shoulders of your chosen network. Your overall network should contain a combination of the following characteristics:

- Supportive elements similar in structure to your family network
- Concentric elements where you are the focal point of the decision making

- Consensus elements where you are part of a team network
- Directive elements where you provide input for consideration to a higher-level network
- Professional association element where you have the ability to access knowledge and information outside of the core group
- Mentor elements where you can seek and receive quality supportive guidance

Your conscious effort to expand your professional network will enhance your professional development in ways that seem unreal. Work toward that goal and experience a new professional learning experience full of opportunities.

Help the team win; all other approaches are destined for failure, for sure.

CHAPTER 17

The Team, the Competition

There is a fine line between team success and individual success and the interrelationship between the two. Organizations compete against each other for customers. These competitions are fierce and sometimes lead to one or more organizations filing for bankruptcy. The business arena is a platform where only the strong survive. Some competitors team up on certain business pursuits to create entities that compete with other titans in the industry. While remaining competitors in other areas, the focus of their joint venture is of primary importance to both organizations as failure in this area will mean failure for both organizations. In the same way, know that you and your colleagues are both competitors and allies. As allies, you work together toward assuring your department's success within the organization and your organization's success in the marketplace. As competitors, you are maneuvering for promotions, job opportunities, funding for professional development, raises, bonuses, achievement awards, performance ratings, and a host of other limited resources available within the organization.

Very few employees understand how organizations financially compensate and how pay raises are determined. The reason is that very few organizations openly communicate their compensation practices. The bottom line is simple. You are in competition for compensation and raises with your colleagues. Your department is in competition for the budget with other departments and so on. Most organizations establish a budget for pay increases and promotions on an annual basis. The amount of the overall budget is typically dependant on how well the organization performed in the prior year and the forecast performance for the following year. This budget is further broken down by organization and department or group. Your raise is determined by how your boss views your contributions in comparison to his expectations and the performance of the other members of your team. In theory, all employees perform to their maximum potential and, therefore, all employees receive equitable compensation and pay increases. In reality, the picture is very different. Employee performances span the spectrum from the unacceptable to exceeding expectations. Note that the bar height is set by the manager and not the employee. Under an effective compensation system, a manager is tasked with ranking employees solely based on expectation fulfillment and overall contribution to the organization's success. Idealistically, these two criterions are one and the same. During the ranking process, good managers place star employees at the top of the food chain and lower-performing employees at the bottom. Great managers work with their employees throughout the evaluation process to assure that no employee falls below their expectation levels by the time the evaluation period ends. Once the ranking process is complete, managers commence the process of allocating shares of the available funds to each employee starting with the high-end performers. The manager is typically provided an average pay-raise budget by the organization based on the total payroll dollar amount for that manager's department. The pay-raise budget is typically in one bucket or lump sum. The organization may impose pay-raise guidelines that the manager is required to consider when allocating the pay-raise funding. These guidelines may include the issuance of standardized increases based on the level of the employee and the rating allocated by the manager. Ultimately, the manager decides how the available funds are allocated. The illustration on the next page represents a very basic tabulation of the process described above.

The bottom line is that you will be compared to your peers and the results of that comparison will determine the rate of your advancement and your financial success. In conflict with this system of evaluation is the fact that, although you and your colleagues are competing for promotions and raises, the only way for anyone to succeed is for the team to succeed.

Self-promotion at the expense of the team will drop your rating and overall standing within the organization. Competition among teammates can create tension and other undesirable effects if the parties focus primarily on themselves and lose site of the bigger picture. Focusing on the success of the organization and performing to the best of your ability, rather than on the group's internal jousting, helps set you apart from the uninitiated. Self-advertisement by leveraging the team's acknowledgements of your performance is the best promotion your career can ever receive.

EMPLOYEE'S PERFORMACE RATINGS AND COMPENSATION FORM				
Employee Name	Performance Ranking (Top performers first)	Recommended Raise (% of Salary)	Minimum Raise Guideline Based on Performance Rating (% of Salary)	Manager's Justification for performance Ranking and Raise Variations from the Guideline
Susan	1	7.1	5.0	Highly promotable. Employee far exceeded expectations and was the top performer for the group.
Jaime	2	6.8	5.0	Promotable. Employee exceeded expectations.
Alfred	3	5.0	5.0	Employee met expectations.
Victor	4	3.0	3.0	Employee completed assignments but required an unexpected amount of guidance and direction.
Kelley	5	2.0	2.0	Employee completed assignments but required significant guidance and direction.
John	6	1.0	2.0	Employee's performance fell short of expectations for the second period in a row. Reference performance review for details.
Cisco	7	0.0	2.0	Employee's performance does not meet the minimum requirements. Reference performance review for details.

The key to succeeding in the team competition is to realize the fact that most professional organizations view team performance as a strong indicator of individual performance. Realize that, although you are in competition with your team for career advancement and financial rewards, the only way to the top is to receive help from your internal competition, your team. Focus your attention on team success, and you will set the course for personal success.

Mentors are only as good as you allow them to become; never place them in awkward situations; always thank them for taking a personal interest in your career.

CHAPTER 18

Mentor Relationships

Professionals rely on checks and balances to ascertain and affirm their approaches, decisions and positions on issues. One of the best ways of jump-starting your professional career is to identify and seek a good mentor, who genuinely takes a personal interest in your success and development. Mentorship programs are designed to provide guidance and direction above and beyond that offered through the employee's management chain. Mentors offer advice only; they do not direct your work. Your boss directs your work. A common mistake that most young professionals make relative to mentorship is that they try to only emulate or become their mentor. Use a mentor as a sounding board for your decisions and approaches to situations. In the end, consider the mentor's advice and make your own informed decision. Be your own person. Set your own course of success. Your mentor is not responsible for solving your problems, for stepping in and saving you from difficult situations, or for placing his or her own career on hold solely to help you with your own career. Mentors are employees of the organization as well, with career paths, reputations, and alliances. Mentors are only as good as you allow them to become; never place them in awkward situations; always thank them for taking a personal interest in your career. Important note: do advise your boss that you wish to participate in a mentor program. Secure buy-in from your boss. Recall that your boss is also your mentor. Great bosses welcome the idea of their employees receiving guidance from another reliable, seasoned, and respected source. Let your boss know your mentor's name. Never give your boss the impression that your mentor questions his or her decisions. Your mentor and your boss are teammates in helping you succeed. Heeding this advice is part of forming a strong professional partnership with your boss and your mentor. Remember, no surprises for your boss.

Identifying and obtaining a mentor is a process that requires thought and purpose. The first step is for you to have a clear understanding of your career goals and aspirations. The second step is for you to identify the individuals that exhibit the kinds of traits and decision-making ability you respect and the organization respects. Another very important factor in the second step is to assure that your mentor's personality is in harmony with and complements your personality. An extremely extroverted person usually does not harmonize with an extremely introverted one. Only you can ascertain whether a particular personality is compatible with your own. The third step is for you to determine if the person or persons you select are capable and willing to become your mentor and for you to follow through to a partnership. You will find that some professionals are great at what they do yet do not possess the skill set and/or willingness to mentor others. A high-level position in the organization does not automatically qualify an individual to be a good mentor nor does it disqualify him or her. Your mentor does not have to be an executive of the organization but should be in a position to guide you through the proven approaches the lead most young professional to successful careers. Gauge your potential mentor's interest and skill as a mentor by gently and respectfully asking for advice on an issue. If the experience is positive for both you and your potential mentor, proceed with asking for additional advice on the same or different issue. Only you will know when and if the time is right to ask your prospective mentor to become your official mentor. At the time you decide to ask another professional to be your mentor, discuss a time frame for the partnership. Usually, twelve to eighteen months is a good starting point. The fourth step is to evaluate your mentorship experience and decide if the partnership is helpful in guiding you to the right decisions. You will know when you have arrived at the right decisions when your decisions create value in the eyes of the organization. Mentor-mentee partnerships are not meant to be forever; some do last a lifetime. There may be situations that you will outgrow your mentor. A good mentor will recognize that you have exhausted his or her help and will assist you in identifying another mentor that can take you to the next level. A great mentor will expect you to surpass his or her accomplishments and be very proud of the fact that he or she was an integral part of your development. If the realization of outgrowing your mentor partnership enlightens you before your mentor, it is very important that you approach your mentor gently. Remember that mentors are people too with emotions. They have a vested interest in their mentees. Your decision to end or significantly limit your professional relationship could backfire. Help your mentor reach the same realization that you are ready for the next stage of your career. The best approach is for you to be genuinely thankful, appreciative, and forthcoming. Ask for his or her help. Talk to your mentor about where he or she has helped you succeed and your career goals. Ask if he or she will help guide you to the next step by recommending another mentor that can provide you with yet another great perspective. Great mentors understand the mentorship life cycle and embrace your willingness to experience the workplace from a different perspective. If you select a mentor that does not embrace the fact that you have outgrown him or her, then your choice of mentor was not the right one. The fifth step is to keep in touch with all mentors because they view your triumphs as their own as well. This action maintains the strong alliances inherently built through the mentor-mentee process.

The following are a few of the characteristics you should be looking for in a potential mentor:

- Highly respected among his peers and throughout the organization
- Impeccable reputation; unequaled credibility
- Exhibits the ability to make the right decisions even if they are unpopular
- Accepts responsibility for his or her actions
- Strong alliances with the team; protects the team
- Ability to encourage the organization to listen
- Exhibits the qualities of a leader, knows when to follow
- Ethical, unbiased, open to diversity in all regards
- Speaks highly of the leadership team, the company, and the customers
- Does the right thing even at his own detriment
- Never questions your boss's decisions or approaches; only provides you with advice on how to best help your boss support the organization as a whole.

Engage in a mentorship program and accelerate your career. If your organization does not offer a formal mentorship program, engage in an informal one. The benefits are rewarding for the mentor and the mentee when the process is properly established, implemented, and understood by both individuals.

---●---

*The best approach while on business travel
is to conduct yourself as if everyone you
encounter has a say into the reputation of your
organization. The fact is that you represent
your boss, your organization, everywhere,
always.*

---●---

CHAPTER 19

Business Trip Etiquette

On occasion, or even frequently, depending on your job, you may be asked to travel for the organization. Your travels may expose you to new places, new cultures, and new people. Know that everywhere you go, and on every encounter, in all hours of the day, you represent the organization. Your actions or inactions including the way you drive, the way you dress, your choice of words, your reactions to situations, your overall demeanor and attitude, the way you treat others, the way you conduct business, and your level of compliance with the requirements of the local culture will impact the way the outside world, including customers, view your organization. This holds especially true when you visibly wear or carry anything that identifies the organization such as an item with a logo. Realize that every person you encounter is a member of a network of people. It is impossible to know the complex connections of the various networks as they interact in a cab car, in a boardroom, at the airport, or at the hotel. Often, the interrelationships of the networks are not apparent until a sequence of events exposes the connection. The best approach while on business travel is to conduct yourself as if everyone you encounter has a say into your reputation and that of the reputation of your organization. The fact is that you represent your boss, your organization, always. The act of handing out a business card is a symbolic affirmation that you are your organization's representative and is conferred with equitable responsibilities. The manifestation of positive encounters is an organizational responsibility bestowed upon you by your organization, yet this responsibility is rarely openly discussed unless there is an issue. Know that part of your job responsibility is to project a positive image of the organization to the outside world. Your selection as a business traveler indicates that your organization trusts and has full confidence in your ability to carry out this responsibility. Undertake ownership and accept the challenge. Do:

- Plan your trip

  - Security requirements and advisories
  - Local points of contact and local access requirements
  - Travel documentation (passport, visa, transportation ticket, etc.)
  - Lodging and meal allowances
  - Local weather
  - Maps/Global Positioning System locations of the local area
  - Daily schedules
  - Meeting agendas
  - Briefings, presentations

- Meet your commitments
- Know why you are on the business trip, contribute, add value

Business trips are an organization's affirmation that you are worthy of representing its image and conducting its business on its behalf. Consider this fact always as a precursor to your adventure.

Excel beyond simply survival. Create and demonstrate insurmountable value to the organization at every opportunity. Become the one the organization cannot be without.

CHAPTER 20

At the End of the Day

Your success or failure in the professional environment is highly dependent on your willingness and ability to read and understand the cards you are dealt, on your approach and timing, knowing when to shuffle, when to play, and when to deal precisely, on knowing when you are the player deciding when to hold and when to fold, on realizing that you are viewed as a resource to help in the growth of the organization, and on your ability to treat the other players as teammates. The kind of resource you chose to become will determine the number of decks you are allowed to control and the number of hands you are allowed to play. Your approach as to the balance between organizational needs and professional needs, strategic thinking and emotional judgment will determine whether you are viewed as an organizational resource full of promise or as a short-term liability. Your courage and willingness to learn the path leading to the point of realization, expectation fulfillment, and perception management are the only limiting factors of your success as a professional. After all, at the end of the day, the passageway to transition and the winding thoroughfare forging professional success are *not intuitively obvious*.

Workbook

Transition to the Professional Work Environment

This workbook is designed to help you navigate through the perception management and expectation fulfillment obstacle course. It is a roadmap tailored for the professional work environment. This workbook is a living document that changes as you change and as the organization changes with you. Year one is your baseline year. You will need to re-baseline anytime you change jobs and/or bosses. The workbook utilizes subsequent years of experience to help you fine-tune the strategic approaches necessary to meet and exceed your objectives. Purposeful and honest utilization of the content will offer you the gift of realization and ultimately the satisfaction of goal achievement.

Year One Baseline

What are your boss's goals and the organization's goals? Ask your boss and develop a detailed list.

_____

_____

_____

_____

_____

_____

_____

_____

_____

_____

_____

_____

_____

_____

—

What are your professional goals? Develop a detailed list.

_____

_____

_____

_____

_____

_____

_____

_____

_____

_____

_____

_____

_____

_____

Describe how your professional goals will help your boss and the organization achieve their goals; be specific.

_____

_____

_____

_____

_____

_____

_____

_____

_____

_____

_____

_____

_____

_____

Describe your plan for meeting and exceeding your boss's and the organization's goals; be specific.

_____

_____

_____

_____

_____

_____

_____

_____

_____

_____

_____

_____

_____

_____

Describe your professional expertise. What are your strengths?

_____

_____

_____

_____

_____

_____

_____

_____

_____

_____

_____

_____

_____

_____

_____

In what areas do you need improvement? Describe your plan for improvement.

_____

_____

_____

_____

_____

_____

_____

_____

_____

_____

_____

_____

_____

_____

What other departments/organizations interface with your department/ organization?

_____

_____

_____

_____

_____

_____

_____

_____

_____

_____

_____

_____

_____

_____

_____

List the ways you can help other departments/organizations understand your job responsibilities.

_____

_____

_____

_____

_____

_____

_____

_____

_____

_____

_____

_____

_____

List the ways you can seek to understand other department's/organization's responsibilities.

_____

_____

_____

_____

_____

_____

_____

_____

_____

_____

_____

_____

_____

_____

Based on what you know about other departments/organizations, list how you can engage and diversify your experience. List the ways in which you can learn more about other jobs.

_____

_____

_____

_____

_____

_____

_____

_____

_____

_____

_____

_____

List at least five ways in which *you believe* you definitively add value to the organization.

_____

_____

_____

_____

_____

_____

_____

_____

_____

_____

_____

_____

_____

_____

_____

How do *you believe* you can add more value to the organization? List at least five ways below.

_____

_____

_____

_____

_____

_____

_____

_____

_____

_____

_____

_____

_____

Ask your boss how you add value to the organization. List the items below.

_____

_____

_____

_____

_____

_____

_____

_____

_____

_____

_____

_____

_____

Does your boss think you can add or should add more value to the organization? If so, describe below.

_____

_____

_____

_____

_____

_____

_____

_____

_____

_____

_____

_____

_____

_____

_____

Compare the previous four questions. Did you identify gaps? If so, describe your plan to bring your perception of value to the organization in-line with your boss's perception of value to the organization.

List the unwritten licenses that are granted to you and why you believe they are granted.

_____

_____

_____

_____

_____

_____

_____

_____

_____

_____

_____

_____

_____

_____

_____

List the unwritten licenses that have expired and why you believe they have expired.

_____

_____

_____

_____

_____

_____

_____

_____

_____

_____

_____

_____

_____

_____

List the unwritten licenses you wish were granted to you and why you deserve them.

_____

_____

_____

_____

_____

_____

_____

_____

_____

_____

_____

_____

_____

_____

_____

_____

_____

Describe the plan that will secure these licenses for you.

_____

_____

_____

_____

_____

_____

_____

_____

_____

_____

_____

_____

_____

List the approaches that have helped you gain the trust of others. List the approaches that have worked against you.

_____

_____

_____

_____

_____

_____

_____

_____

_____

_____

_____

_____

_____

_____

_____

List the approaches that have helped you build a good reputation and those that have harmed your reputation.

_____

_____

_____

_____

_____

_____

_____

_____

_____

_____

_____

_____

_____

_____

List the approaches that have helped you build strong alliances. Why did these approaches work?

_____

_____

_____

_____

_____

_____

_____

_____

_____

_____

_____

_____

_____

_____

_____

_____

List the approaches that have discouraged alliances. Why do you think these approaches did not work?

_____

_____

_____

_____

_____

_____

_____

_____

_____

_____

_____

_____

_____

_____

Who do *you think* are your internal and external customers? Make a list. Who does your boss say are the internal and external customers? Do these two lists match? If yes, you are aligned with your organization. If not, more work is required, develop a plan with your boss.

_____

_____

_____

_____

_____

_____

_____

_____

_____

_____

_____

_____

_____

What do you think are the internal and external customer expectations? Does your boss agree? If yes, you are aligned with your organization. If not, more work is required, develop a plan with your boss.

_____

_____

_____

_____

_____

_____

_____

_____

_____

_____

_____

_____

_____

_____

List the ways in which you meet your internal and external customer expectations. Does your boss agree? If yes, you are aligned with your organization. If not, more work is required, develop a plan with your boss.

_____

_____

_____

_____

_____

_____

_____

_____

_____

_____

_____

_____

_____

_____

List the ways in which you do not meet your internal and external customer expectations. Describe the plan that will turn this around. Does your boss agree on your approach? If yes, you are aligned with your organization. If not, more work is required, develop a better plan with your boss.

_____

_____

_____

_____

_____

_____

_____

_____

_____

_____

_____

_____

_____

_____

_____

_____

—

What are your boss's expectations including pet peeves (do not ask your boss)?

_____

_____

_____

_____

_____

_____

_____

_____

_____

_____

_____

_____

_____

_____

What are your boss's expectations including pet peeves (ask your boss)?

_____

_____

_____

_____

_____

_____

_____

_____

_____

_____

_____

_____

_____

_____

List how you meet your boss's expectations and also how you do not meet your boss's expectations. Consult your boss.

_____

_____

_____

_____

_____

_____

_____

_____

_____

_____

_____

_____

_____

_____

What is your plan for addressing any gaps between what you think your boss expects and what your boss actually expects?

_____

_____

_____

_____

_____

_____

_____

_____

_____

_____

_____

_____

_____

_____

List your accomplishments. Link your accomplishments to your boss's goals and your organization's goals.

_____

_____

_____

_____

_____

_____

_____

_____

_____

_____

_____

_____

_____

_____

—

List the areas where *you think* you need development/improvement. Obtain your boss's input.

_____

_____

_____

_____

_____

_____

_____

_____

_____

_____

_____

_____

_____

List how *you think* your boss would rate you and your teammates in order of performance with the top performer at the top of the list.

_____

_____

_____

_____

_____

_____

_____

_____

_____

_____

_____

_____

_____

_____

—

List the reasons why you perceive the top person is at the top of the performance list in the eyes of the organization. Describe your plan to reach the top or to stay at the top. Does your boss agree that your plan will improve your performance?

_____

_____

_____

_____

_____

_____

_____

_____

_____

_____

_____

_____

_____

_____

List every person that knows you professionally; internal and external to your organization.

_____

_____

_____

_____

_____

_____

_____

_____

_____

_____

_____

_____

_____

List the professionals that should be on the previous list (network expansion). Describe your plan to grow your network.

_____

_____

_____

_____

_____

_____

_____

_____

_____

_____

_____

_____

_____

_____

_____

List your teammates. By each one of their names write the word *introvert* or *extrovert* or *neither*. Include yourself. Additionally, place a check mark by those you get along with the most. Place a check mark by those *you feel* are the top performers. Place a check mark by those *you respect* the most. Place a line through those whose performance hinders the organization more than it helps (*your perspective*). Finally, circle those who *you feel* the organization favors consistently.

_____

_____

_____

_____

_____

_____

_____

_____

_____

_____

_____

_____

Do you see any correlation between the personalities, those you get along with well, perceived performance levels, and the respect factor? Do you see any correlation between those the organization favors, their personalities, approaches, and performance? Explain any correlations and perceptions. Explain the actions you can take to help your team improve relationships.

What are the most important mentor traits from your perspective? Be specific.

_____

_____

_____

_____

_____

_____

_____

_____

_____

_____

_____

_____

_____

_____

_____

—

What do you expect out of a mentor-mentee partnership? Be specific.

List possible candidates for mentors and their position within the organization and explain why you consider them to be a potential mentor for you.

_____

_____

_____

_____

_____

_____

_____

_____

_____

_____

_____

_____

List your potential mentor's expectations of the mentor-mentee partnership. The list should be mentor-specific. Compare this list with the last three lists and determine if they help you select a mentor that compliments your needs.

_____

_____

_____

_____

_____

_____

_____

_____

_____

_____

_____

_____

_____

Describe the image your organization requires you to convey during a business trip and/or during interactions with the paying customer.

_____

_____

_____

_____

_____

_____

_____

_____

_____

_____

_____

_____

_____

_____

_____

Describe the actions you need to take to assure that the organization's image expectations are met before, during, and after your trip and/or customer interaction.

_____

_____

_____

_____

_____

_____

_____

_____

_____

_____

_____

_____

_____

_____

Do you consider yourself to be an invaluable resource to your organization? Does your boss agree? If so, explain why and provide detailed examples. If not, explain your plan for reversing the perception.

_____

_____

_____

_____

_____

_____

_____

_____

_____

_____

_____

_____

_____

What specific reasons does the organization have to either hire you or to keep you on the payroll? Are there any reasons for the organization to let you go? Be honest with yourself. Your ability to recognize the amount of value assigned to you by the organization is dependent upon your willingness to determine, understand, and formulate a realistic answer.

_____

_____

_____

_____

_____

_____

_____

_____

_____

_____

_____

_____

Year Two and Beyond

Look back a year at the composition of your team. Do you still have the same team members today? If not, list those that are no longer in your group and the reasons why they are no longer a part of the team. Are you part of the same team? If not, explain. If yes, explain why you believe you are still a member of the team. Review your previous personal ratings of the team members and that of your own to determine if there is any correlation that explains the team membership now verses the team membership last year. It is highly unlikely that you will be surprised of what you discover. Does the organization value your performance contribution more now than it did last year? If not, what is your plan for immediate improvement?

_____

_____

_____

_____

_____

_____

_____

_____

_____

Review each answer in year one and evaluate your progress. Develop a plan for improvement for each area where there is a gap or a change in perceptual direction. It is expected that your answers will change as your career matures. Your responses will positively transform as the result of your growth and transition to the professional work environment.

NOTES

NOTES

NOTES

NOTES

NOTES

NOTES

___

NOTES

NOTES

NOTES

Notes

NOTES

NOTES

NOTES

NOTES

NOTES

NOTES

NOTES

Notes

NOTES

Notes

NOTES

NOTES

The professional guidance continues . . .

J. A. Rodríguez Jr.

Not Intuitively Obvious
Transition to Leadership

The second book in the series is written to assist professionals' transition from individual contributors to effective leaders. The field of view or perspective of a potential leader must broaden to capture more than simply exceeding organizational goals. Responsibilities expand beyond those of self and into organizational performance, career development for subordinates, external customer interaction, and role model responsibilities. Enhanced perception management skills are a requirement with little room for error. With a lifetime of experience behind every chapter, this comprehensive book is a must-have for all who demand the odds of excelling to be on their side.

COMING SOON

Visit www.notintuitivelyobvious.com

About the Author

J. **A. Rodríguez Jr.** is a senior manager for a Fortune 200 company. He has over twenty-six years of professional work environment experience. The last twenty-one years of experience are in leadership roles of increasing responsibility. His responsibilities extend to the development, deployment, and implementation of strategic plans and programs across the globe for creating partnerships in new and existing business initiatives and for supporting billions of dollars worth of active contracts, spanning over hundreds of U.S. and international sites.

Prior to his current position, Rodríguez has served in several professional capacities in the areas of environmental, health and safety compliance, quality assurance/performance excellence and quality control, ethics compliance, U.S. Department of Defense Security processes, and engineering management on a nationwide technical services contract as a member of the leadership team. He is well versed in the areas of management, engineering, services, construction, and emergency preparedness.

Before joining his current employer in January 1989, Rodríguez served as a senior engineer in the nuclear power generation industry. While there, he led a team of professional engineers and subject matter experts in the identification and application of electrical engineering solution sets.

Presently, Rodríguez is a professional member of the American Society of Safety Engineers, a professional member of the Board of Certified Safety Professionals with a designation of Certified Safety Professional (CSP), a United States Department of Labor Occupational Safety and Health Administration Voluntary Protection Program Special Government Employee (SGE), and has passed certification examinations in the area of business continuity planning. Other professional affiliations have included the National Fire Protection Association, Institute of Electrical and Electronic Engineers, American Society for Quality, and

Occupational Safety and Health Administration Outreach Training Program (Construction and General Industry).

Rodríguez holds an associate in engineering degree in electronics engineering technology from Wentworth Institute of Technology in Boston, Massachusetts, and a bachelor of science degree in electrical engineering from Western New England College in Springfield, Massachusetts. In his professional career, he has developed a significant number of comprehensive courses; has personally delivered hundreds of training seminars as an expert instructor and compliance advisor; has managed, mentored, and motivated teams of professionals; has coached and advised company leaders in the technical services, engineering, construction, and manufacturing industries; and has taught college level electronic engineering courses as an adjunct professor.

Rodríguez has demonstrated international expertise in the rehabilitation of enterprise safety performance through the development, implementation, and utilization of effective process-oriented management systems. His strategic and tactical methodologies have contributed to significant performance improvements on programs worldwide. He is recognized as a dynamic and motivational speaker and a foremost expert in the areas of construction, electrical engineering, safety and health regulations and compliance, and health and safety legislation analysis.

Rodríguez is an author, inventor (patent no. 5,285,961), martial arts instructor, musician, and motivational speaker.

For more information about the author or to contact the author, visit

www.notintuitivelyobvious.com

ACKNOWLEDGMENTS

A universe of gratitude to

Iluminada Rodríguez, my loving mother, and Arnaldo Rodríguez, my brother, who taught me never to accept defeat as an option and devoted their lives to their profession.

Isaac A. Rodríguez and Kayla M. Rodríguez, my children, who inspired me to write this book and were tremendously helpful in its development and promotion.

Kristi A. Rodríguez, my wife, who gave up family time so that I can accomplish my dream and provided invaluable support and input.

G. Gary Maxwell, Capt, USN (Ret), for his military perspective and guidance on the approach.

My family, who provides me with a grounded structure always.

Jeff Cardin, who is always there for me and provided insightful input.

SGM Jimmy W. Mills, U.S. Army, who provided his military perspective, assistance, and support for this book.

Mike Cleary, who provides an outlet for ideas and a vehicle for encouragement. His friendship and generosity are second to none.

Jim Bonner, who shares with me the seemingly impossible quest for the perfect lawn.

My employers, who provided me with the fertile ground for growth and opportunity.

My bosses: William Britz, who undertook the challenge of my youthful mistakes and remained firmly by my side; John Hall, who provided over a decade of immeasurable leadership and mentorship; and Steve Biello, who, looking back, had enough faith in me to risk his reputation by promoting a young gun through to the senior manager ranks. My goal is to always make you all proud.

My mentors: Joan Moosally, for the leadership and true friendship; Peter Dascanio, for the unwavering guidance and support; Dan Schultz, for the leadership, devotion, team approach to the job, and the infectious drive to always deliver more than you think you can. My hope is to always assure that all of your efforts light the way for others as well.

Xlibris Corporation, my publisher, for making this book project virtually effortless.

The following world-class learning institutions for providing me with the quality education that has allowed me the opportunity to pursue professional employment for over twenty-six years:

Wentworth Institute of Technology, Boston, Massachusetts

Western New England College, Springfield, Massachusetts

Strayer University, Fredericksburg, Virginia

The following world-class learning institutions for providing my children with the quality education that will allow them the opportunity to apply the lessons learned in this book to their professional careers:

University of Virginia, Charlottesville, Virginia

University of Minnesota, Minneapolis, Minnesota

Virginia Commonwealth University, Richmond, Virginia